ALWAYS
ADVANCING

ALWAYS ADVANCING

Modern Strategies for Church Growth

by
R. Daniel Reeves
and
Ron Jenson

A Campus Crusade for Christ Book
HERE'S LIFE PUBLISHERS, INC.
San Bernardino, California 92402

ALWAYS ADVANCING: Modern Strategies for Church Growth
by R. Daniel Reeves and Ron Jenson

A Campus Crusade for Christ Book

Published by
HERE'S LIFE PUBLISHERS, INC.
P.O. Box 1576
San Bernardino, CA 92402

ISBN 0-86605-120-1
Library of Congress Catalog Card 83-073128
HLP Product No. 403188
© 1984 by Campus Crusade for Christ, Inc.

Manufactured in the United States of America.

To my wife Ethelwynne
—closest colleague,
partner and friend,

Dan Reeves

To my wife Mary and my children Matt and Molly
—who teach me how to love life.

To Dr. Earl Radmacher, Grant Howard and Loren Fisher
—who taught me how to love the church.

Ron Jenson

The Authors

R. DANIEL REEVES

Dan Reeves received his bachelor of arts degree from Westmont College in 1966 in social science and business administration. In addition to his two graduate degrees in church growth from the School of World Mission in Pasadena, Dr. Reeves has more than fifteen years of practical experience as evangelist, mission executive, pastor and teacher, in England, France and the United States. He has published articles in the *Church Growth Bulletin* and *Church Growth America* and continues to carry out research on the cutting edge of the church growth science. For several years he has worked cross-denominationally in the areas of congregational diagnosis, master planning, conflict resolution and problem solving, and has conducted special church growth seminars. He is presently providing supervision for mid-career consultant interns as well as serving as a consultant at the Charles E. Fuller Institute in Pasadena, California.

RON JENSON

Ron Jenson received his doctorate in 1974 from Western Conservative Baptist Seminary in Portland, Oregon. To research discipling in the local church for his doctoral dissertation, he visited 175 of the leading churches in America, traveled 20,000 miles in 37 states and interviewed over 300 leaders in these churches. For nine years he served on the pastoral staffs of two churches—one rural and one suburban—and was the dean of a church leadership training center. He is currently president of Church Dynamics, a church-growth consulting and development firm; president of the International School of Theology, a seminary for developing church and para-church leaders, with campuses on three continents; and executive vice president of the International Christian Graduate University.

ALWAYS ADVANCING

Modern Strategies for Church Growth
by
R. Daniel Reeves
and
Ron Jenson

TABLE OF CONTENTS

TABLE OF ILLUSTRATIONS

FOREWORD

Part of the excitement of being in the Church Growth Movement is to observe how God continues to provide for its development. Piece by piece, new insights are surfacing and new books are written. *Always Advancing* expresses this well by the title itself. It is a slogan that can apply to both the Church Growth Movement in general and your local church in particular.

Daniel Reeves and Ron Jenson are thinking mostly in terms of how this all translates into ministry in the congregation. The excellence of this book emerges from the heartbeat they both have for fulfilling the Great Commission and the broad background they have in the Church Growth Movement. Reeves provides the perspective of both scholar and practical church growth consultant (an "ecclesiologist") while Jenson adds personal anecdotes from his experience as pastor and motivator of seminary students. It is a winning team and the book they have produced is clearly a winner.

One of the special new contributions of this book is the chapter on paradigms. Church growth leaders have long recognized the fact that unseen psychological obstacles seem to prevent some from grasping the validity of church growth principles. This chapter dispels the fog and explains why it happens. It also helps us understand what happens to those church leaders whose ministry is radically changed during a church growth seminar—

they have undergone a "paradigm shift."

Other extremely helpful insights of the book include the material on "people flow," philosophy of ministry and typologies. Church workers at every level will benefit from understanding that God loves churches of an enormous variety of hues and stripes, and that He brings unchurched persons into them through diverse means. This is the first time these matters have been explored in such depth in church growth literature. You will find it fascinating.

This is not all. Throughout the book Reeves and Jenson have combined the old and the new into a solid, dynamic and readable book. **It is a basic church growth primer, the book you will want to give away as a concise introduction to the field.** It will be read and acclaimed both in North America and in the Third World. For Christian leaders, clergy and lay, it will stimulate interest, fire up the imagination, build biblical faith and furnish practical suggestions for implementation toward the growth of the church.

—C. Peter Wagner
Fuller Seminary School of
World Mission
Pasadena, California

PREFACE

Some may ask with legitimate concern, "Why another book on church growth?" It is a necessary question because of the proliferation of literature using the term church growth since 1974. According to the most recent estimates, more than 400 books relating to church growth concepts have been published worldwide. Of these, 50 were written by Americans for use within North American churches. In addition, several new books have been released more recently which demonstrate an unprecedented depth of understanding of the complex reasons some churches grow while others decline.

The answer to the question can best be stated by isolating two important factors with respect to each of these previous publications: (a) *the intended target audience,* and (b) *the extent of accumulated data.* Once this has been achieved at least six observations can be made concerning the status of church growth literature at the present time:

1. Many of the authors have written exclusively about the experiences of a *single church* or a *single denomination.* These books are invaluable because they take the reader inside a living church or family of churches for a glimpse of the problems and the potentials present at the local level. Because they are specific in scope they provide concrete models of ministry which interested outsiders can analyze to a considerable extent. The insights

11

gained can be applied to those congregations able to relate to the experiences explored.

2. Many of the books were intentionally written to focus on *one particular aspect of church growth.* Some authors, for example, have researched the problem of declining membership, or have pursued the challenge of planting new churches. Others have offered constructive suggestions for overcoming the difficulties related to heterogeniety, or those caused by lethargic, immobilized members. Each of these efforts has provided church leaders with helpful guidelines for avoiding various pitfalls and for harnessing untapped potential.

3. Most of the authors have limited their academic research to a *representative portion of the available literature.* Because of their intent to motivate pastors and lay persons into specific actions, the approaches in most instances have been entirely appropriate. An exhaustive study would have bored their readers and overwhelmed them with an unnecessary amount of detail.

4. Many of the books were written with only a *minimal understanding of the insights* being collected by more than 750 research associates *at the School of World Mission* in Pasadena. In a few cases omission of these insights was intentional, but in the majority of instances it was due to a lack of opportunity to integrate these concepts through a concentrated period of study.

5. Of the mid-career professionals who have studied in Pasadena, most have carried out their research *in countries outside North America,* and have focused their attention on helping churches in other lands. Until recently, this tendency has been encouraged by the rigid cross-cultural entry requirements and by the faculty's priority of commitment to churches in the Third World.

6. Most of the American church growth literature to date has been written *to the non-professional.* In some cases this was due to what was perceived by credible authors as an audience with an otherwise limited sales

potential. In the majority of instances, however, it was caused more by the urgent need to equip both laity and clergy with practical tools in evangelism, discipleship and leadership development. Many of these are written in the style that claims, "This is how we do it," or "Here are the basic principles of church growth that often can be applied universally." These resources have filled the training vacuum to a great extent during recent years and will continue during the 1980s to meet needs in a high percentage of American churches.

On the other hand, this textbook is the first church growth publication which attempts to relate the isolated parts of American church growth into a *meaningful whole.* It is intended to be an integrated, introductory perspective for the serious student at the Bible college or seminary level. In addition, it has been designed as a *resource textbook* for professional pastors who have neither the time nor the inclination to digest and integrate what more than 50 self-appointed church growth spokesmen in America are emphasizing.

Certain decisions had to be made at the outset in regard to the length and scope of the contents which follow. Because American church growth is located at the crossroads for several disciplines in the behavioral sciences, in theology and in history, the choices have not been one dimensional. Understandably, some individuals will not be pleased with the arbitrary limitations placed on material within their areas of expertise. Even among church growth professionals there undoubtedly will be disagreement with regard to proportions, since boundaries for this rapidly emerging discipline have not been clearly established.

We assume that the person who studies this text enjoys reading and will want to read further after completing this survey of basic concepts and available resources. The intent is therefore to consolidate, to provide focus, and to indicate specific directions for further study.

The experienced reader undoubtedly will notice that many of the classic sources prior to 1970 have been omitted from the "best book" biographies. While contemporary thoughts may not always represent the most accurate perspective, the insights they bring are drawn from broader data, and can be more usefully applied to present issues. Consequently, we have preferred contemporary texts of outstanding quality over more detailed sources.

—The Authors.

ACKNOWLEDGMENTS

In regard to the thoughts contained in this book we are deeply indebted to Donald McGavran and Peter Wagner. Their burning convictions about the church of Jesus Christ in the last two decades of this century not only served to light our candles, as a rite of passage into the church growth movement, but to invest the next 30 years of ministry carrying the torch and igniting churches with this same fervor.

We also want to acknowledge our deep gratitude to Samuel Southard who together with McGavran and Wagner provided the encouragement necessary to complete this project. And finally, our appreciation goes to Alan Tippett, Ralph Winter, Charles Kraft, Arthur Glasser, Paul Hiebert, John Wimber, Carl George and Win Arn, each of whom provided helpful input at various points during the six-year development of this manuscript.

CHAPTER ONE
Principles of Church Growth

The challenges related to church growth are not new to our age. The New Testament is filled with letters from Paul, Peter, John and others who encouraged the various churches to expand their membership, to do more witnessing to unbelievers, and to support the work of missionaries and evangelists.

Today, the reasons for church growth have not changed from those same reasons established long ago by the apostles. What *has* changed, however, is the variety of problems facing today's church and the methods of dealing with those problems.

Truly, times have changed. When the apostles focused on church growth, they had to deal with such problems as the Roman suppression of Christianity, the routine imprisonment of church leaders, and the on-going confrontations Christians were having with the Jews.

How different these problems were from such current challenges as planning church budgets during times of rising inflation and high unemployment, dealing with cults, and trying to maintain an active local church body in a society in which 20 percent of the population moves to a new neighborhood or new city each year.

The methods used in fostering church growth are different today, too. The public speech and the hand-carried epistle were adequate forms of communication during

the times of Peter and Paul. The population was small.
We are now in an age of microchip data banks, word pro-
cessing machines, satellite relay television networks, and
microwave telephone lines. Today, the population has
become immensely expanded, but technology has provided the potential for the Church to continue to reach
everyone.

In essence, the need for church growth is as obvious
as ever. The challenges facing church growth have
changed, but so, too, have the ways of facing these
challenges. Hence, the reason for this book. Once
pastors, deacons, Sunday school teachers, directors of
calling programs, and members of congregations learn
how to plan, initiate and carry out an effective church
growth strategy, the subsequent growth of the Church
will be rapid and continuous.

GROWTH PRINCIPLES

As noted, a continually important issue in Christendom
today is the church growth movement, particularly in
view of the attention it has generated during the past
decade. There is no all-inclusive answer to the question
of how church growth can best be achieved. Nevertheless,
there are specific principles which are indispensable,
conscious-raising concepts that are vital to the health
of the church.[1]

Research reveals that most church leaders are unaware
of many of the factors which contribute to the growth
pattern of their organization. Ask them why their church
is growing and they will respond with a typical statement
such as: "We work, pray, and love" or "God promised it
would happen" or even, "We just preach the Word and
everything else falls in line."[2]

And while unwavering faith is surely what God would
have every church show, this must be accompanied with

works. So it is then, when you examine a church that is experiencing growth, you discover that it is applying certain principles that usually insure growth—*even if the church leaders do not recognize these principles as theories-in-action.*

Many of the successful principles which these growing churches follow were formulated more than six decades ago by Arthur Flake.[3] Put in a modern situation, however, "Flake's Formula" and all other lists of church growth principles can be reduced to six basic factors. Let's examine them briefly:

1. *A Common Purpose and Philosophy*

Almost without exception, growing churches have a sense of destiny. They clearly understand certain biblical mandates which serve as blueprints for action. Though many have no written purpose, their members are clear about their objectives. Most important, members are consistent in regard to mission. They are in agreement about the task to be done, and their definition of mission is conveyed effectively to new members.

But if churches have been clear on *what* their purpose is, they seldom have been equally as clear on *how* to go about achieving that purpose. Usually they lack a philosophy to be guided by. This can lead to vacillations in church expansion rather than a steady growth continuum.

Those churches which do formulate a philosophy of ministry generally make it a successful one by having it integrate the seven most needed elements: namely, the pastor, the congregation (people), the community population, the national church boards (polity), the church's statement of purpose, its programs, and even its problems (see Figure 1).

In determining how to blend these seven factors so that they work most effectively in each individual church setting, a profile of the particular church involved must be

Figure 1

PHILOSOPHY OF MINISTRY CONSTRUCT

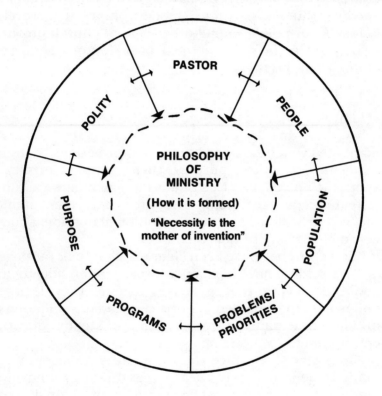

Source: Adaption of Models Developed by Fuller Evangelistic Association,
        Department of Church Growth, 1977

prepared. In effect, a church must first analyze its *self-image,* then define the *specificity* of its mission and then reach decisions about the *strictness* of its disciplines and restrictions before it can expect to apply its newly-formed philosophy and achieve results. Let's review some points about these elements of a church profile.

Self-image. Growing congregations invariably possess a clear identity, a positive image that reaches out to include new members. This good self-image is often accompanied by a friendly, contagious attitude that sees neighbors as "brothers" before leading them to be "believers." Visitors to church often will be greeted with smiles, hugs, and sometimes even brotherly-love kisses.

Specificity. Churches which have learned that God speaks at different times to numerous persons in varied ways have a stronger philosophy of ministry than those who speak to each other in general or borrowed terms. Calvin described the church as "a place where the Word is proclaimed, sacraments administered and discipline maintained."[4] Television preacher Robert Schuller has tailored his reformed theology remarkably with his new definition: " . . . a group of joyful Christians happily sharing their glorious faith with the despairing souls of their fellowmen who have never known the joy of Christ."[5]

Similarly, James Latimer has demonstrated specificity during his conferences. His answers to questions are concrete and definite, establishing his credibility and lending authority to his ministry. The high impact of his message parallels a highly specific philosophy.

All dynamic movements, when analyzed, will evidence that they have a clearly stated outline of purpose and philosophy which is focused on encouraging church growth.

Strictness. Churches are often quite varied in their attitudes about strictness regarding doctrine, membership, baptism, and service. Some churches have high membership standards based on aggressive and unapologetic theology. Such congregations usually exclude those who do not conform to the teachings of the church. Furthermore, they expect members to serve readily and to live by strict spiritual and moral tenets. Other churches encourage membership and church involvement, but they are not adverse to having Sunday-only attendees. Such churches feel that something positive is accomplished if they can just get members of the community to attend services willingly and regularly. In this manner, they at least have an opportunity to share the Word with a larger number of people.

Though degrees of strictness may vary from one local church to the next, it is important for each church to be aware of its stance. Otherwise, it will be extremely difficult to execute the newly formed church ministry philosophy.

2. *Effective Leadership*

Those who study church growth factors will usually cite strong, effective leadership as the key to continued successful results. When a church has a senior pastor who functions as a pacesetter and is supported by energetic and competent staff and lay leaders, that church invariably experiences growth.[6] Developing such a team of leaders is a challenge, however, and expanding it is a never-ending effort (see Figure 2).

Scripture does *not* restrict contemporary congregations to a narrow range of leadership styles or structures. Therefore, effectiveness must be a primary consideration in the selection of any leader or leadership philosophy.[7]

The pastor who is to be an effective leader must have certain qualities and talents. Lee Lebsack rates faith, vision, personal passion for the lost, and hard work as indispensable pastoral qualities.[8] Win Arn points to a willingness to take a risk as a good trait.[9] C. Peter Wagner says a pastor must be a man who has clearly defined objectives and the ability to evaluate candidly the results

Figure 2

LEADERSHIP VS. MEMBERSHIP

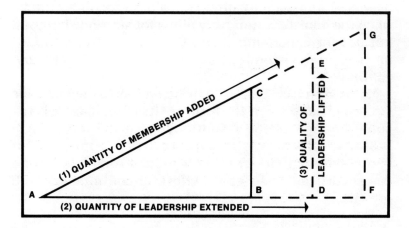

of his plans and procedures.[10]

Although not widely recognized among effective pastors, *longevity is another factor in church growth. Generally, it takes a new pastor seven to twelve years to energize an established congregation. In some cases, such as the fastest-growing Assembly of God churches, the average stay of pastors is twenty-two years.*

One of the chief difficulties with pastorates of three or fewer years is that the congregation often undergoes a change just when the most productive years of a pastor are about to begin. Generally, long-term pastoral commitments, including associates and assistants, are extremely positive characteristics.[11] The major exception occurs among rapidly growing younger congregations, when the minister is uniquely gifted for starting churches, but not for expanding them. Overall, the trend toward much shorter pastorates, started during the 18th century, continues.[12]

Multiple church leadership is being proclaimed in some circles as the wave of the future.[13] Its main feature is the subordination of the senior pastor to the level of co-pastor or elder. This may prove to be a mistake for churches which are eager to have a strong leader who can spearhead a successful effort for continued church growth.

3. *A Mobilized Membership*

A mobilized membership may be a more important factor in church growth than even a strong pastor; yet, while most churches recognize the need for programs to recruit and train additional lay persons, relatively few are pleased with the results. The difficulties relate to such fundamental questions as how many and who to train, where they should work, and how they should minister. Some of the best answers to these questions come from growing churches that have discovered their own effective combinations.

Section A of Figure 3 shows that most available church volunteers lack the interest and the necessary qualifications for effective front line ministries with unchurched persons. Even in growing congregations, leaders are unable to mobilize consistently more than one out of five persons for evangelism or outreach projects. About forty percent of the members in growing churches are not at all involved in the ministry at a given point in time. These "consumers" are benefactors of the work performed by the other sixty percent.

The reason this unbalanced workload is so detrimental is because the typical healthy urban congregation has a medium lifespan of only seven to ten years. In that perspective, the awesome limits of time and energy quickly become apparent (see Section B, Figure 3).

In understanding the total problem, consider this: volunteers who concentrate on tasks that benefit present members and those who focus on activities which benefit outsiders donate from three to ten hours per week, whereas the consumers spend no more than one to three hours in church each week. Only five percent of the congregation's members spend ten or more hours each week involved in church services and activities. Considering this, it is both amazing and encouraging to discover that, despite such minimal resources, growing churches are still able to fulfill many of their evangelistic obligations.

The reason for this success is related to the employment of plans and systems which are often as effective as the target marketing strategies of Madison Avenue advertising agencies, even if done on less grandiose levels.

Although churches employ a variety of means to recruit, the process usually includes an immediate involvement of new Christians with peers, meaningful nurture and spiritual growth and, above all, the presence of skilled leaders who know how to transfer responsibilities by inspiring confidence and injecting enthusiasm. Effec-

Figure 3

MEMBERSHIP MOBILIZATION
IN GROWING CHURCHES

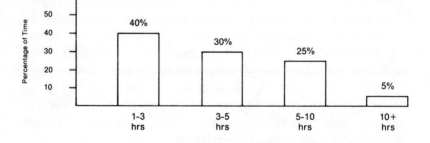

A. Average Distribution of Work

B. Average Time Availability

Source: Composite ratios from
        various workshops and
        consultative studies, 1977-1980

tive mobilizers are highly committed individuals who are driven by a compulsion to encourage and support others.[14]

An additional observation of time management studies of mobilized churches reveals that they emphasize *role specialization.* Volunteers are placed in jobs according to their interests, aptitudes and suitability rather than on an arbitrary or availability basis.[15] They are often taught that according to Romans 12, 1 Corinthians 12, and Ephesians 4, God's will for them includes discovering, developing, and using their spiritual gifts in local church ministries. This specialized development of workers also rests upon the biblical conviction that excellence should be rewarded. "Do you see a man skilled in his work? He will stand before Kings; He will not stand before obscure men" (Proverbs 22: 29). This procedure can result in developing volunteers who are committed to developing their spiritual gifts.[16] Motivating and training a person according to his or her gifts takes less time and energy and often leads to increased happiness, fulfillment, and effectiveness.

A final means of mobilizing congregations was learned about after pastors had analyzed the situations of members who were no longer active in church affairs. These so-called "lapsed members," representing approximately one-third of most congregations, usually had psychological, emotional and/or rational needs which were not being met. With proper care and understanding, it was found that programs could be created which revitalized and reactivated them.[17]

4. *Multiple-level Commitments*

In recent years sociologists and ecclesiologists have raised questions concerning the internal structures of congregations. Most congregations develop the ideas and ideals of the core of people who are most actively involved in the creation of the local body. During the first six months, the tendency is for small exclusive groups to develop within the leadership. This is normal and healthy so long as other groups are being formed continuously and the leadership circle remains approachable and dynamic.

This process of Christian psychotherapy within the membership circle fulfills the needs of the smaller church in a variety of ways. Most people need a small support group for confidentiality and accountability but a larger body of forty to sixty persons for identification. As the congregation grows beyond 120 members, however, sub-congregations need to assume increasing responsibility for identification and belonging.

There does not appear to be a numerical limit to the size a church can grow while still being able to respond adequately to the human needs of intimacy and belonging. The Full Gospel Church in Seoul, Korea, for example, recently passed the 100,000 mark and is still growing; yet, its complex, highly personalized structure provides all the benefits of a smaller church.

An example of how one southern California church analyzed the structure of its main internal organizations is seen in Figure 4. All groups were studied for purpose, size, frequency, and effectiveness in ministering to the unchurched. The results assisted the elders in determining the type and number of new groups that were needed.

In general, congregations need to assess their structural progress periodically at four levels. The *friendship level* is where the deepest interpersonal relationships are experienced between two or three persons. The *support group level* relationships are developed among eight to fourteen persons. The *subcongregational level*—usually between forty to eighty persons—offers further fellowship and a deeper sense of belonging. The *worship level,* with no numerical limits, provides spiritual nourishment and unity.

Figure 4

INFRA-STRUCTURE ANALYSIS
Membership Involvement in Major Activities

**ACTIVE
MEMBERSHIP (300)**

⬡ – Choir
▭ – Adult Fellowships
▢ – Bible Studies
△ – Monthly Gatherings
◯ – Other Activity Clusters

La Habra Hills Presbyterian Church

The principle of "multiple-level commitments" suggests that a large church should strive for a balanced involvement in all four areas. Normally, growing churches
involve about forty percent of their members at the support group level. Whereas involvements at the subcongregational level are not necessary for smaller
churches, in larger bodies the subcongregations comprise approximately forty percent of the membership.
More than any other factors, satisfactory multiple-level
commitments produce the momentum-building quality
of *contagiousness.*

5. *A Balance Between Evangelizing and Nourishing*

To sustain a steady rate of church growth, a balance
between conversions and discipleship is needed. According to McGavran, churches tend to want to take care of
what they have, rather than become involved in
evangelizing the lost.[18] For continued church growth, the
nurturing of believers toward maturity needs to be
balanced with on-going evangelistic programs. Since
most churches emphasize "feeding the flock," concentrated efforts are needed to discover effective, consistent
outreach strategies rather than rely on random or spontaneous evangelism.[19] Planned evangelism, together with
purposeful discipleship, will encourage church growth.[20]

6. *Linking the Congregation to the Community*

For many congregations, linking the church with the
community is the least understood and the most difficult
principle to apply. Nevertheless, its relevance to growth
is undeniable. The proposition simply stated is this:
*Growing churches are able to match their resource
capabilities with the spiritual and sociological realities
and needs in the community.* This process involves knowing oneself, knowing one's neighbor, and then bridging
the gap. According to Ezra Earl Jones, " . . . few
judicatories (agencies) have done area surveys and

developed strategies through which each local church can understand itself and its relationship to other congregations and the larger community."[21] Although some hopeful signs of progress in this area have surfaced in recent years, most congregations still fail to see opportunities in the community to fill needs. Instead, they continue to respond only to crisis situations.

One of the problems in the community-church relationship is the "ours is a friendly church" syndrome. Insiders invariably perceive themselves as being warm and outgoing. Outsiders often do not agree with this assessment. What is friendly to one group can be viewed as cliquish by others. Peter Wagner calls this "people blindness," the failure to recognize communicative differences between people.[22]

Growing congregations have discovered the keys that unlock the doors between themselves and their neighbors. They have found people who are responsive to their approaches. Sometimes churches use the "shotgun" method to secure unity and cohesiveness between themselves and their community. At other times, they have discovered success through research and testing. When programs are successful, strategies can be refined and approaches modified for greater effectiveness.

Solomon said, "Where there is no vision, the people perish" (Proverbs 29:18). It is evident that a solid leadership philosophy and a positive church image is necessary for continued church growth. Outside resources, planning, goal setting, and consistent motivation are some of the management tools available for this process. If used with wisdom, these procedures produce a challenging, exciting ministry, and transform the vision of successful church growth into reality.

Footnotes for Chapter 1

1. For a list of collections containing church growth principles, see Appendix B.

2. Hogue, 1977:22; Martin, 1977:8.

3. Flake, 1922. Known as "Flake's Formula," this list of "how to" steps for building a Sunday school is still widely respected in Southern Baptist circles. The sequence is ideal for effective assimilation by lay leaders: (a) know your possibilities; (b) enlist and train workers; and (c) go after the people.

4. Calvin (incomplete source)

5. Robert Schuller, 1974:60.

6. Werning, 1977:391.

7. For additional pastoral resources on the subject of effective leadership, see Adams (1978) and Regsdale (1978).

8. Lee Lebsack, 1974:115.

9. Win Arn (McGavran and Arn) 1977:105.

10. C. Peter Wagner, 1976:30-32.

11. Schaller, 1977:53-54, 1978:25-27, 56, 60 and Wagner, 1976:62-63.

12. Of the ministerial graduates at Yale College from 1702 to 1775, 79 percent served one parish only throughout their lifetimes (Carrol 1977:7, 77, 82). Regrettably, career mentality has produced a ladder syndrome in which small churches are staffed for the most part by the youngest or oldest ministers, or recent entrants.

13. See, for example, Getz (1974:121-122) and Moore (1978:14).

14. One of the clearest processes is suggested by Neil Brown (1971:128-132). A more recent formulation is contained in Douglas Johnson's, *The Care and Feeding of Volunteers* (1978:35-53). See also Minor (1972) and Huber (1975).

15. Snyder, 1975:125-127.

16. Spiritual gifts resources are at last plentiful. By far the most popular text interdenominationally is Wagner (1979b). An excellent motivational film has been produced recently by the Institute for American Church Growth, 150 South Los Robles, Pasadena, CA 91101. And a variety of materials and workshops are available from the Charles E. Fuller Institute, 44 South Mentor, Pasadena, CA 91102. See

also, Bridge (1974), Murphy (1975), and Yohn (1975).

17. Three of the most helpful sources on this subject are Savage (1976), Werning (1977:64-85), and Schaller (1978:115-121).

18. McGavran, 1955:33.

19. McGavran and Arn, 1973:171-172 and 1977(?):55.

20. For further study see Henrichsen (1975), Hartman and Sutherland (1976), McPhee (1978), and Johnson (1978).

21. Jones, *Strategies*, p. 150. It should be noted that in 1983 the Church of Christ began to use computers to develop neighborhood and community demographies to help determine in which locations new churches should be built.

22. C. Peter Wagner, *Your Church Can be Healthy* (Nashville: Abingdon, 1979), p. 53.

CHAPTER TWO
Growth Procedures

It is often difficult to distinguish between the established rules for church growth and the means by which to implement those rules. The procedures for promoting growth are varied and must be selected and analyzed carefully to determine suitability. Let's get an overview of the major elements related to church growth plans.

1. *Resource Management*

Choosing the right management tool to increase church growth can be a confusing dilemma for many pastors. Although approaches may vary, common administrative questions recur. "Which resources are the most reliable?" "What are the alternatives?" "How much time and money will be involved?" "How do we get started?"

It takes time, aptitude and determination to be able to provide proper management for a growing congregation. It is imperative that a competent "strategy chief" be appointed—one who can create effective "game plans." If the leadership finds denominational planning procedures unavailable (or perhaps unacceptable), the interdenominational approach developed by Edward Dayton might be considered[1] (Figure 5). This eleven-step cyclical plan was created for international use, but its application to American churches has proven to be highly effective.

Figure 5

The Process Of
MANAGING CHURCH GROWTH

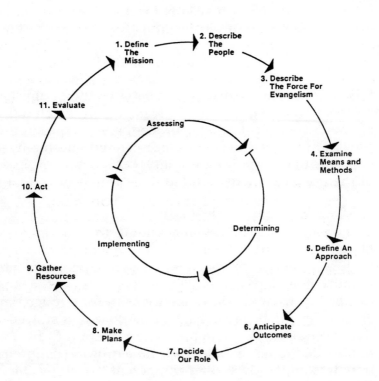

Source: Adapted from Dayton (1978)

Setting priorities often creates tension between maintenance and innovation. "Every congregation . . . must concern itself with both the purpose for which it is called into being and maintenance of the institution developed to support it."[2] The balance may shift briefly, but one side of the scale must not be allowed to permanently outweigh the other.

The most difficult decisions for management spring from establishing priorities for the use of internal resources. Choices must be made between several service options: foreign missions and local evangelism; renewal and church growth; consultation fees and self-help research materials; singles, youth, and senior citizen ministries.

Imbalanced financial allocations may threaten the success of planning. Priority conflicts can arise over the real or imagined need for more staff members. Many churches have built large sanctuaries and have then been forced to meet the mortgage payments by "borrowing" funds set aside for the new staff allocations. Other churches have hired staff workers prematurely, before having sufficient facilities.

Even more common is an imbalance caused by a lack of vision. Planning committee conservatives are not always in accord with faith leaders. However, persistent optimism usually is enough to counteract overly cautious, inflexible planners.

2. Composition Awareness

A growth concept that relates directly to effective procedures is the homogeneous unit principle (HUP). In order to describe the way the majority of people become Christians, McGavran developed the axiom, "People like to become Christians without crossing racial, linguistic, or class barriers."[3] Individuals join churches and become responsible Christians in cultural units known as *peoples.*

It is imperative that churches in urban centers of

America understand the realities of people movements and homogeneous units. Without such insights, growth efforts can be critically hampered. America's rich cultural composition lends itself to one-on-one evangelism. If this is neglected or ignored, many hidden peoples (such as the 50,000 racetrack residents or the 130,000 recently arrived Vietnamese, or the several million white, single, swinging apartment dwellers) may remain unreached.[4]

3. *Research Procedures*

Research can reveal the difference between present realities and future possibilities. Growing churches describe research tools as the "cutting blades" of their harvest machinery. Churches which spend considerable time and energy in promoting ineffective evangelism are trying to harvest without having their cutting blades in place.[5] Failure to adjust programming, in light of the current knowledge of growth patterns and available research tools, represents a tragic waste of resources.

Soil testing (a term borrowed from American agriculture) has become a useful procedure. It involves determining areas ripe for high spiritual response. Three regions have proven to have high growth potential: (1) growing churches; (2) people in the process of change; and (3) concentrated areas of lower middle income blue collar workers. For example, in southern California where growing churches are abundant, harvest strategies should be based on the number of receptive unchurched persons within a reasonable driving distance.

Receptivity is a primary element in the McGavran gauge known as the *resistance-receptivity axis.* The left end of a horizontal line represents groups with high spiritual resistance, and the right end represents those with high receptivity. Units of people such as aerospace workers, young single adults, and recent Cuban arrivals are placed at points along the bar. Those who fall in the middle are considered indifferent. Research has shown that people who are resistant will not respond to any approach, whereas those who are receptive will respond to nearly any reasonable approach. Most groups fall somewhere between these extremes. Successful church growth strategies should develop programs that will reach the more responsive people.[6]

Most denominational headquarters provide research materials for both external and internal studies. Research procedures should include surveying the community population for size, density, and the capacity for expansion or decline. Life-styles and life-situations also reveal trends and provide a knowledge base for creating effective projects.[7]

4. Using Consultants

Occasionally, when needs arise, professional consultants are available to assist congregations with research and planning. Any decision to use a consultant should be weighed carefully against the need, the availability of internal persons, and the overall expense. As professional helpers, consultants are able to offer practical, objective advice concerning the vital signs of church health. Consultants clarify trends, determine needs, and aid congregations in reaching their potential. With services designed to fit any church budget, consultants can bring clarity and harmony to the growth process within a period of one to three years.[8]

The following list of questions is suggested for churches considering the use of a consultant:

(1) Can our current budget handle the cost of a professional consultant?

(2) Do we already have people in our congregation who are knowledgeable about advertising, direct mail campaigns, door-to-door canvassing, newspaper and radio publicity, and special promotions?

(3) Should a revival service or an extra week of vacation Bi-

ble school or a Sunday school contest be experimented
with first, before we hire a consultant to help us draw
new people to our church?

(4) What particular problem areas would we want a consultant to help us find solutions to?

(5) Can we find other churches in our area whose leaders
can tell us about the results they obtained after hiring
an outside consultant?

5. *Goal Setting*

Goal setting naturally follows trend assessment and
precedes programming. Goals aid growth in four major
ways. First, *they provide direction.* The Apostle Paul said,
"I run in such a way that I might win" (1 Corinthians
9:24-27). He knew where he was going and what his
results ought to be.

John Henry Frosbre, French naturalist, has done
research on the processionary caterpillar. If put end to
end around the circumference of a flower pot, these cater-
pillars follow one another until they are exhausted. They
do what churches so often do: confuse activity with
accomplishment.

Second, *goals inflame imagination.* The Bible, especially the New Testament, is a source book of creative ideas
for churches and schools to follow. When faith is applied
to goal setting, God comes on the scene. More than any
other procedure used during the last twenty-five years,
churches have been helped most by looking at their ten-
year graphs, praying, and then setting five-year goals.
It is a phenomenon that is partly spiritual and partly
rational.

Third, *goals motivate and direct people away from
wandering generalities and toward meaningful specifics.*
If the church sets a larger faith goal, God gives more
power to meet the need. Faith becomes the substance
of things (goals) hoped for and the evidence of things not

seen (Hebrews 11:1). Goals help the statements of purpose and philosophy become unified for something specific. They switch the focus from the past to the future and move congregations in a designated direction.

Finally, *goals expand potential.* If fleas are put in a can with a lid on it, they will jump up and hit the lid. When the lid is removed, they will still jump only as high as the cover. Tradition is often the lid that keeps the church from expanding its potential. In one church, a singles ministry grew from eight people to 150 in six months because the leaders began to make big plans, pray unceasingly, and act as if God had already met the need.

In addition to outreach goals, internal objectives are necessary. Such things as organizational aims which relate to staff and facilities, and nurture goals which coordinate worship, education and fellowship, and mobilization projects which deal with training and evangelism are all very important. Satisfactory goals must be measurable, manageable and relevant. The acrostic AIMS defines the process well. Goals should be *A*chievable, *In*spirational, *M*easurable and *S*hared.

6. *Needs Assessment*

Successful goals should help to define the churches prime objective—to meet spiritual needs. According to Robert Schuller, "The secret of a growing church is so simple—find the hurt and heal it."[9] This may necessitate changing from a message-based approach to an audience-based approach. Both Jesus and Paul used this method, in contrast to the long-winded Pharisees. Paul said, "I have become all things to all men so that by all possible means I might save some" (1 Corinthians 9:22, NIV). Audience-directed programs question, "Is anyone out there listening?" or "Do you understand what I am trying to say?" They avoid general, abstract or irrelevant presentations.

While remaining true to their biblical message, churches which are sensitive to congregational needs will use varied methods to share the message. One church in the Northeast conducts services only on Saturday evening to accommodate its target audience, single adults. Following the example of Luther and modern African missionaries, many worship services now use a vernacular Bible translation. To counteract growing illiteracy rates, Sunday school curricula closely parallel the popular children's program, "Sesame Street." One of the major challenges in the latter quarter of the twentieth century will be how to remain strong in principle while becoming more flexible in programming.[10]

7. New Unit Strategies

Churches expand and extend their range by forming branch and regional churches. When national denominations "plant" new churches, their overall growth increases. Afterward, when these individual congregations start their own branch groups even more growth occurs.

But, this principle can work negatively as well as positively, particularly when new units are formed *inside* a church. When Sunday school classes combine, for example, their vitality and growth potential are reduced; similarly, when congregations and denominations merge, growth rates begin to slow down.

Successful unit division, whether for extension or expansion purposes, should respect homogeneous groupings. Denominations may start individual ethnic churches (house churches) or develop "mega" churches (clusters of subcongregations). Effective leaders in both cases share the same characteristics—they are goal oriented, highly motivated, and blessed with spiritual gifts. Dr. Cho, who pastors a congregation of 225,000 people each Sunday morning in Seoul, Korea, intends to have a half million people in his church by 1990. Thousands of small groups in his church continue to divide and then use the same type of leadership found in a church of a thousand in the United States.

There are nine basic extension strategies: parenting, satellite, multi-congregational, brothering, colonizing, district team, catalytic, fusion, and task force.[11] Any of these approaches can be used individually or in clusters. Whichever method is used, it is important to create a positive division climate and to select and train enthusiastic leaders.

8. *Motivation*

Internal and external transformation involve modifying the attitudes and behavior patterns of a total system. McGavran concludes that this change comes slowly, not by organizational pressure, but by the dissemination of ideas. Leaders must speak reasonably and progressively when and where it matters.[12] Sociologist Alvin Pitcher recommends such complimentary leadership styles as "the 'insider' who persuades and the 'outsider' who pushes."[13] Pastors, lay ministers, and outside consultants all can play a part in church transformation.

Leaders who wish to innovate change have to be dynamic, imaginative personalities who are set aflame with a love like that explained in 1 Corinthians. They also must be skilled in personal relations. By using resources, research, goal setting and motivation, they are able to face the essential issues and determine what to graft, what to create, and what to preserve. With divine help, growth obstacles and weaknesses are overcome, leaving the church alive and healthy.[14]

Footnotes for Chapter 2

1. Edward Dayton (1978)
2. Ezra Earl Jones, *Strategies for New Churches* (New York: Harper and Row, 1976), p. 55.
3. McGavran (1970:198)
4. The definitive work on the subject, and one which is particularly useful as a "consciousness-raising" device for pastors and lay leaders in America, is Wagner (1979b). See also McGavran (1970:183-215), Yamamori and Taber (1975:9-56), and Driggers (1977).
5. Engel and Norton (1975:13)
6. For the theological basis of these convictions see McGavran (1970:255-258).
7. For one of the more helpful and compact series, see Hogue (1977:149-156) and Chaney and Lewis (1977b); for suggestions concerning lifestyle and situation, and for more feasibility studies see Jones (1976:53-54, 58-94). For the theory of understanding one's community, see Warren (1965). Two other resources, both in the mainstream of church growth, are Waymire and Wagner (1980) and Smith (1976).
8. For further general information about consulting practices, see Lippitt and Lippitt (1978:1-44).
9. Robert Schuller (1974:4)
10. For practical suggestions on needs assessment programming, see Belew (1971:70-79) and Neighbour (1975).
11. A brief description of these is contained in Orjala (1977:107-115).
12. Change can also occur by divine intervention. Numerous instances are recorded in Orr (1973, 1974, and 1975).
13. Schaller (1972:83)
14. Tippett (1973b:145) and Barnet (1953:42, 313-323)

CHAPTER THREE
Growth Problems

Environment is as important to churches as it is to plants. For something to be able to live and grow, it must be in a healthy environment.

An executive once bought a beautiful exotic potted plant for his office. Each day he gave it water and set it in the sunlight. At the end of two weeks the plant had lost six leaves and was turning brown. The man was dumbfounded. He called the florist to complain.

"Have you used a spray bottle to mist the plant each day?" asked the florist.

"No," admitted the man. "Why should I?"

"Without a warm and moist environment, the plant will die," he was told.

The man began to mist the plant regularly. Within days it was strong again and beginning to sprout new leaves and flowers.

Churches also need healthy environments if they, too, are going to grow. This chapter will focus on some of the problems churches have which often lead to unhealthy growth environments.

In a very real sense, the study of church growth is as exact a science as medicine. Church growth diagnosticians, like physicians, perform tests, draw conclusions and then prescribe remedies. Though not all church diagnosticians use the same analysis tools or speak with the same terminology, the procedures are generically very similar.

The problems facing American churches are usually referred to as being *entropic* (internal erosions of growth due to death of members, families moving to new cities, and other similar circumstances) or *non-entropic* (outside elements such as economic depressions or societal shifts which have an impact on church growth). We will now examine both of these problem umbrellas to discover the varied factors under each one.

ENTROPIC PROBLEMS

In a normal state, churches are to be living, dynamic, and fruitful. Yet there are forces of decay, almost from the inception, which begin to sap their strength and vitality. Other forces can delay or even counteract those which destroy. In the physical sciences the second law of thermodynamics establishes that a change from an ordered state to a less ordered one is inevitable. Most social scientists believe that living organisms are subject to this entropic law as well. All current research indicates that expanding churches are not immune to its power:

> Once a Christian movement has reached its peak of expansion, instead of maintaining a high plateau of spiritual life and activity, it normally tends to 'cool off.' Not that people return to the same level of religious response as before the 'revival' or 'movement'; but they may well become 'lukewarm' about a new faith. There is nothing essentially strange about this reaction; it is typical of all human movements, religious or otherwise (Nida 1960:150).

Entropy is a principle cause of *nominality.* The latter is an inclusive term for such symptoms described by leaders throughout the ages as powerless religion, formal faith, intellectualized Christianity, and apostate church. Many contemporary pastors insist that nominality is the greatest problem facing churches today. In subsequent discussions nominality will refer to someone who is as follows:

> . . . a religiously indifferent person who perfunctorily performs the formalistic rituals of the Christian faith. In his ambivalent state of mind he superficially adheres to a diluted concept of God which issues a powerless religious performance on a few fixed church occasions. With his double-minded, half-hearted allegiance he is one of the fringe members of the Church who has more in common with the world than with Christ (Buehler 1973:1, 17-18).

This condition is seen in the message to the church of Laodicea in the Book of Revelation. There, the author says, "I know your deeds, that you are neither cold or hot; I would that you were cold or hot. So, because you are lukewarm and neither cold or hot, I will spit you out of my mouth" (Rev. 3:15-16). Entropic forces are the central cause, not only of nominality, but of a significant cluster of other conditions plaguing American churches. Furthermore, these forces have been overlooked in recent U.S. history, just as they were in ancient Israel, during the age of the early Church and throughout the expansionary phases of Christianity. Entropy, then, shows us that "all other things being equal, any group activity will in time tend to diminish in intensity, since familiarity with the patterns of behavior results in loss of dynamic impact" (McGavran 1976a:173).

a. *Carnality.* As a cooling mechanism, entropy has varied but overlapping dimensions. Each adds excess weight to churches which results in a loss of energy. *Carnality* is the word often used to describe the first of these dimensions. It is a *spiritual cooling.* As members lose the excitement of a Christ-centered life, church growth becomes retarded. Appetites of the flesh pull against the spiritual nature of Christians. Soon, their Christian values are replaced by secular values. There can also be a lack of faith in God and the Scriptures and an unwillingness to obey among members. They have been properly taught, but they are not experiencing the powerful realities of spiritual commitment.

b. *Second generation slippage.* All churches, even those with gifted founders and devoted followers, find it difficult to transmit the ultimate meaning of their convictions to those who are not experienced enough to ask the right questions. Each generation must discover and develop its own theology. As the core of active "old-line" disciples diminishes, a feeling of nonchalance gradually sets in among the less committed. Homesteaders, for example, do not often share the same heritage as pioneers. The identifying factor in this type of energy loss is the *age of the local congregation.* The most critical period is from 20 to 30 years after a church starts. If a congregation has relocated, the time begins after the first services are conducted in the new facilities.

c. *Institutionalism.* The more developed a church becomes, the greater amount of energy it requires to keep it running smoothly. Spontaneity is gradually replaced by *structure;* self-imposed disciplines are exchanged for legislative *standards;* faith tends to evolve into *creeds,* which in turn become mere *recitation. Maintenance* begins to take precedence over mobilization; concern for the lost is substituted by concern for *edifices.* Institutionalism produces boredom and dissatisfaction. It contributes heavily to church dropouts, because members desire a warmth and acceptance that bureaucracies cannot easily provide.

One of the authors recalls a pastor, whom he was consulting, relating the story of his experience in one denominational church. He had been called to this church as a young pastor to stimulate new life in the church; or so he thought. However, as he began to lead a number of people to Christ and started to bring them into the church, there was some concern by some of the deacons of this church. During one meeting, the head deacon leaned over to the pastor and said, "You must stop bringing these new people into *our* church. We've been happy with this church for years and we don't want it changed!" The new converts were predominantly younger and some of them were rather unconventional in appearance. This was very disturbing to the older deacons. They simply wanted to maintain the status-quo. They were not interested in growth. Later, the pastor baptized seven people one evening whom he had personally led to Christ. The deacons became so enraged, they fired him. That's institutionalism.

d. *Extended Success.* Strong Christian convictions often wane under the pressures of success, increased exposure to other cultural lifestyles, and materialism. As rewards for diligence and zealousness, these worthy elements compete for the allegiance of church members' affections. Without the presence of counter forces, the seeds of failure (which are produced as a result of extended success) become mighty plants that eventually threaten the survival of the garden. Although the data are conflicting between church trends and upward mobility, most research indicates that individuals who are affected tend to drop out rather than join a more liberal church.

e. *Exclusiveness.* Internal structures normally cool and solidify over time. The effect for churches is the erection of invisible barriers that cause new persons to feel excluded. This particular variety of entropy has several manifestations. There are leadership groups, for example, which become ingrown. Sociologists refer to this inner core as a *primary group.* New leaders, though assigned authority, often feel left out and cut off from those who hold the real power. Exclusiveness is also caused by the *fears of hard driving legalists* who by the force of their personalities preserve conservative values and drive away other potential leaders.

An additional contributing factor to exclusiveness is *age.* In a congregation where the median age of the adult membership exceeds 50, or the median tenure for present members is higher than 15 years, or more than 15 percent of the adults are surviving spouses, the potential for growth is substantially reduced. As with other levels, group cohesiveness among older members is both a strength and a weakness. The same ties which provide security and nostalgia also erect exclusiveness barriers for those who cannot share their memories.

Churches that have become accustomed to their only pastor usually demonstrate exclusiveness when a second minister is hired. All churches suffer from exclusiveness in varying degrees. A spiritual cure is found in Luke 22:25-27: "The beneficiaries must become the benefactors"; a structural cure is found in beginning new supportive units.

f. *Ecumenism.* Among the highest aims in many churches is to develop an ecumenical spirit at the grass roots level. However, as noble as intercongregational cooperation may appear, its real results for participating churches are a decline in individual church identity and strength. Church growth and cooperation are built on incompatible forces. Ecumenism has a restricting effect upon congregations because it diffuses limited resources along divergent paths. It often is rooted in what McGavran calls *parallelism*—a belief that all mission activities are of equal value.

A good example of this over cooperation was Key 73. This was an honest attempt to try to spur evangelism, but everybody got involved in various universal programs which blurred their own distinct images. As a result, it did not have near a great impact. Contrary to this was the involvement in the Here's Life program in America and throughout the world today. The "I Found It" campaign has met with varying degrees of success throughout the United States and has been universally successful overseas. A major reason for the success was that though it mobilized various churches in a community, it allowed for churches to maintain their own programs and conduct their own followup.

NON-ENTROPIC PROBLEMS

The above six categories all have in common a downward pressure that causes a loss of systemic vitality. But at least eight other recurring problems can be classified as *non-entropic.* In other words, their causes cannot be linked to the cooling processes endemic to congregations. Entropic and non-entropic forces have an equally inhibiting overall effect upon churches.[1]

a. *Culture.* Ethnocentrism is a widespread phenomenon in American churches that stems from a misunderstanding of culture. Largely unconscious, it insists that "our way is best." Ralph Winter's interpretation of Christianity as an historical movement is strongly tied to this concept. He calls it the "uniformitarian hypothesis"—a belief that if people would just see things as "we" do, the world's problems would be solved. Misunderstandings involving value systems have led historically to more than just arguing and fighting. They have also prevented the unchurched from finding their way into Christian congregations. Barriers are erected needlessly over questions of dress, vocabulary, recreation, music and literature. Sociologists describe the force as a misguided *assimilationist philosophy;* popular writers label it *cultural chauvinism;* Peter Wagner calls it *people blindness.*

One fellowship which has been successful at understanding its public is the Calvary Chapel ministries in California. The Calvary Chapel mother church in Costa Mesa, pastored by Chuck Smith, has generated hundreds of other churches and anticipates starting thousands more in the near future because it has developed a unique type of church geared toward a particular clientele. The leadership of these various churches understands well the needs of people from teenage years through their thirties in America today and has learned to accommodate the right type of ministry, including the music, worship, social activities, and teaching, appropriate to that group. These churches are pastored by young men who have usually gone through the training and exposure at the mother church. They have caught the vision of understanding a certain clientele and knowing how to minister to it.

Two other problems related to culture are *gradualism*—McGavran's term for maintaining a prolonged presence in difficult circumstances, even though evangelistic efforts are consistently ineffective—and *homogenization,* or acculturation, where one kind of group imposes its values upon certain parts of another group. In this latter case, the result is often the stripping away of cultural identities so that individuals are incapable of later relating as missionaries to others of their kind.

b. *Change.* Four different problems arise from change. *Urban change* produces symptoms that city planners refer to alternatively as *white flight, urban blight,* or *city decay.* Sociologists of religion emphasize the word change in their analyses of this condition because it is caused by enormous cultural shifts. As is commonly known, churches of the inner city have been devastated during the recent decades by shifting communities. Anglo-Americans moved to the suburbs in droves, leaving behind congregations unable to adapt to the conditions surrounding them. Many such churches have faced "death with dignity." In a growing number of instances, forms of ministry now flourish on the sites where others perished. Regrettably, a large proportion of churches afflicted by the disease are unaware that it is almost always fatal. About one third of the nation's churches are affected by it.[2]

Rural change has a vastly different effect upon churches than does urban change, where the migrations are outward rather than inward; in rural areas the people most involved in change are the youth, rather than the ethnic sectors. However, both urban and rural changes have one disturbing factor in common: namely, a *terminal condition.* Churches cannot grow where migrating groups are not replaced. More than 10 percent of America's churches have been afflicted by rural demographic shifts. Wagner terms the disruption *old age.*

During the late 1970s and early 1980s when the automotive market was in such a slump, many laid-off auto workers moved to Texas, Oklahoma and Arizona (the "Sun Belt") where new jobs were available. The well-established churches in such automotive cities as Detroit, Flint and Kenosha suffered greatly when their congregations and offerings dwindled.

Another fluctuation that affects both urban and rural church is a *change in age.* Here a slight migration occurs in both directions simultaneously. Youth between 18 and 30 tend to drop out, mostly for local contextual reasons, while families with grade school children tend to return.[3]

Changes in leadership are also a disruptive factor in congregations of every type. In a growing church the growth rates drop typically for a period of three to five years following a change in pastor. At least five to eight years are usually required in stable or declining churches before a new minister, even one with a high church growth profile, can reach his potential.

Space. A final problem due to change is listed separately, because it is the only difficulty which, ironically, results from implementing effective church growth strategies. A lack of *space* occurs when congregations outgrow their facilities. Like all other forms of life, churches require space in order to be healthy and fruitful. Space problems are caused by the failure of church leaders to adequately anticipate and prepare for growth. Claustrophobic tendencies begin to appear gradually once a congregation fills at least 80 percent of its sanctuary or parking lot or other major facilities. The symptoms become critical when during peak hours new persons do not return for discomfort reasons alone. This causes churches to suffocate.

Pastor Robert Schuller had such a problem once with parking. Rev. Schuller tells the story of sitting on the 14th floor of the Prayer Tower at the Garden Grove Community Church (or the Crystal Cathedral as it is now called). On this particular Sunday morning he saw one car come in and drive around the entire parking lot and then go out the far exit and leave the church because there was no place to park. This grieved his heart because he thought that this car represented an individual, or a family who might not know Christ or might need help at this time. He brought up this concern in his meeting with his board the next week.

As the men entered the board room that evening, Rev. Schuller was sitting there looking distraught and downtrodden. As they asked him what was wrong, he slammed his fist down on the table and shouted, "GENTLEMEN, YOU ARE NO LONGER IN CHARGE OF THIS CHURCH." There was absolute silence. And then he said, "AND I AM NO LONGER IN CHARGE OF THIS CHURCH." And then he shouted even a bit louder, "AND GOD IS NO LONGER IN CHARGE OF THIS CHURCH!"

The men were bewildered, but Schuller went on to say, "The parking is in charge of the Church!" He continued with this sense of drama and he made his point about a need for parking. This resulted in the purchasing of 10 acres for $100,000 each. One million dollars, just for parking. Schuller would agree today that that was one of the wisest moves he ever made; he *had* to make it: they were experiencing sociological strangulation.

Research confirms that church size is not in itself a significant factor in church growth. It is neutral. Facilities, however, appear only to affect churches adversely. In other words, too much space does not in itself produce growth. But facilities can choke off new growth by not providing sufficient space.[4]

Footnotes for Chapter 3

1. For a fascinating study of how whole denominations (national institutional factors) have been affected by entropic pressures, see Greeley (1972) and Richey (1977). Significantly, these theories, as well as Kelley's well-publicized view on strictness, have survived the scrutiny of empirical research by those with vested interests in proving them false (Hoge and Roozen 1979:345-351).

2. For further treatment of churches in change, including case studies, see Driggers (1977), Jones (1976:151-154) and DesPortes (1973).

3. Because of the variety of ways in which age is used by different researchers, its relationship to entropic diseases is confusing. A quick review shows two age problems in each category: (a) age of church (20⅓), entropic-second generation slippage; (b) median age of adult members (50⅓), entropic-exclusiveness; (c) youth leaving town, non-entropic (rural change); (d) youth dropping out, non-entropic (age cycle).

4. Two other variables which relate to facilities are *style* and *place*. Architectural style can be a positive or negative force depending upon the target audience. Studies concerned with human ethnology have determined that place is far more important than previously believed. See Schaller (1979:69-92) and Deasy (1974). For other works dealing with church problems see Dittes (1967) and Neighbour (1972).

Best Books on Growth Principles, Growth Procedures and Growth Problems

The 16 most insightful books on practicing American church growth are listed below:

1. ANDERSON, James D., and Ezra Earl Jones
      1978 *The Management of Ministry*, Harper and Row, San Francisco.
2. BARTEL, Floyd G.
      1979 *A New Look at Church Growth*, Faith and Life Press, Newton, Kansas.

3. CHANEY, Charles L.
   1982   *Church Planting at the End of the 20th Century,* Tyndale, Wheaton, Illinois.
4. DUBOSE, Francis M.
   1978   *How Churches Grow in an Urban World.*
5. GIBBS, Eddie
   1983   *I Believe in Church Growth,* Eerdmans, Grand Rapids, Michigan.
6. JENSON, Ron, and Jim Stevens
   1981   *The Dynamics of Church Growth,* Baker, Grand Rapids, Michigan.
7. JOHNSON, Douglas W.
   1978   *The Care and Feeding of Volunteers,* Abingdon, Nashville.
8. JONES, Ezra Earl
   1976   *Strategies for New Churches,* Harper and Row, New York.
9. McGAVRAN, Donald and Winfield C. Arn
   1981   *Back to Basics in Church Growth,* Tyndale, Wheaton, Illinois.
10. McGAVRAN, Donald and George G. Hunter
    1980   *Church Growth Strategies That Work,* Abingdon, Nashville.
11. MALLISON, John
    1978   *Building Small Groups in the Christian Community,* Renewal Publications, West Ryde, Australia.
12. RICHEY, Russell E., ed.
    1977   *Denominationalism,* Abingdon, Nashville.
13. SCHALLER, Lyle E.
    1983   *Growing Plans,* Abingdon, Nashville.
14. WAGNER, C. Peter
    1979a *Your Spiritual Gifts Can Help Your Church Grow,* Regal, Glendale.
15. 1979b *Our Kind Of People,* John Knox Press, Atlanta.
16. WALRATH, Douglas Alan
    1979   *Leading Churches Through Change,* Abingdon, Nashville.

CHAPTER FOUR
Prescriptions and Pathways

Having outlined the entropic and non-entropic problems, we'll now look at some solutions to those problems. We'll also examine "people flow pathways" which help congregations identify both their growth limits and growth capabilities.

Prior to that, however, we should note that the approach taken in this book regarding church growth problems of specific natures (size, location, history, finances) does not ignore spiritual or doctrinal problems. However, research has shown time and again that doctrine alone does not build or unify churches.

In general, less than 20 percent of all Protestant congregations are bonded firmly by doctrinal issues. Churches with poor doctrine can do well growth-wise, as evidenced by the rapid proliferation of cults. Conversely, churches with solid biblical doctrines may show a decline in growth, due to any of the problems previously mentioned. Church growth advocates feel that the best growth formula is good doctrine plus good strategy. Churches showing real growth have pastors and people with a high commitment toward biblical evangelism.

Let us now examine ways in which these growth efforts can be assisted.

I. GROWTH PRESCRIPTIONS

When faced with slow growth situations, congregational leaders typically respond in one of three ways: they
resist change; they *regroup* their people; or they *reformulate* their program. In some instances local churches
react in all three ways. Although one response usually
proves to be better than the other two for most churches,
it is sometimes necessary to experience all three before
discovering the one which is most effective.

1. *Resistance*

It is normal for congregations to resist change. Like
any living organism, a church has several instinctive
responses designed to protect itself. Among the most
common is the tendency to *justify* and *defend.* Rather
than recognize the signs of poor health, congregational
leaders often will take the offensive. In some instances
this will involve attacking the credibility of statistics contained in trend assessments; in other cases, leaders will
argue against or dismiss the evidence.

An example of this rationalization was seen in an article in *Christianity Today* some years ago that said that
the rate of decline of a certain denominational church
had equalized. Do you understand what actually was said
there? The point was that the church was losing members
at a steady rate rather than a sporadic rate. It was still
a bad situation, but it had been termed in such a way
that it appeared to be positive. That's self-deception, a
hiding from reality.

Congregations must be willing to evaluate themselves
honestly. If a person who looks sideways into a mirror
sees that he has a huge stomach then turns to face the
mirror, does that mean the weight problem has gone
away? Of course not. Similarly, if churches play word
games with their annual attendance reports it does not

change the fact that the congregations are losing members. Reality can be resisted for just so long and then it becomes too obvious to disguise.

Another frequent response is to *ignore* the evidence. By doing nothing, leaders avoid having to make painful decisions. There often is an underlying hope that trends will somehow correct themselves. Among churches with a high percentage of "conservatives," following the path of least resistance usually seems to be the most attractive alternative. Procrastination and "stonewalling" become major deterrents to growth. A related response, and one that is equally retarding, is the shifting of attention to the past, when things were more prosperous. By doing this, values are preserved and facing reality is temporarily postponed.

Often church members and leaders, fearing failure, will ignore current evidence of a dwindling congregation and will seek, instead, to celebrate the past. This general fear of failure is a cowardice that is rampant in society today and is even evident in the church. Someone has said, "You don't test the response of God until you attempt the impossible." This is the kind of daring mentality that is sometimes needed in today's churches. Congregations need risk takers, people who are willing to go out on a limb even though they may fall.

Robert Schuller has said, "I would rather attempt something great for God and fail, then attempt something insignificant for God and succeed." That has been very evident in his life style and in his willingness to risk putting together something that was, at least at its inception, universally ridiculed: the Crystal Cathedral in Garden Grove, California. Building this multi-million dollar structure was truly a daring undertaking. Whether you agree with the necessity or even wisdom in building such a structure is beside the point at this juncture. What *is* important is Schuller's willingness to attempt

something great for God. It took courage, the kind of
courage that needs to be rekindled throughout the body
of Christ and particularly in church leaders.

2. *Regrouping*

Only certain difficulties trigger responses that require
total *regrouping.* The two most common problems are
a lack of *space* and situations of *urban change.* For congregations overwhelmed by shifting population, the decision is often made to move the church to the suburbs.
Although this is not the church's only option, it is the
one that initially appears to have the most advantages:
peace, prosperity, new ministry opportunities, increased
growth potential, and congregation survival. However, by
relocating, some congregations merely exchange one set
of problems for another. These difficulties frequently include an initial reduction in the resource base (leaders,
finances, and workers), improper site selection, overconfi-
dence in the ability of a new building to attract new members, a lack of consultation, and transportation problems.

The most common reason for relocation is a lack of
space, brought on by a congregation which has outgrown
its facilities. Here the problem is not *community turmoil*
so much as *community inflation.* Land is considerably
less expensive in growing suburbs than in fully developed
cities. Even though the same obstacles must be con-
fronted by "overgrown" churches as by "overrun"
churches, the economic temptation to most is often irre-
sistible.

In addition to relocation, four other forms of regrouping sometimes occur: (1) formation of *satellite congregations,* either with a view to relocating in stages, or as a
means of solving present space problems; (2) *sharing of
resources,* such as staff, programming and facilities, with
one or more churches, usually in the same denomination; (3) *merger* of two or more churches; or (4) *disbanding*
of a site where property is sold and all resources are chan-

neled into other existing ministries.

There are a number of interesting examples of satellite congregations that are being developed by various churches today. One experiment is the Calvary Chapels that began in Costa Mesa in the 1960s to meet the need of the "Jesus people." This congregation has grown into several hundred churches and anticipates having as many as a thousand in the future. The churches have developed satellite relationships and have had a dynamic impact upon area communities.

Another interesting model was developed by Bob Ricker at Grace Church in Edina, Minnesota. Pastor Ricker and his staff of elders carefully evaluated the region around their metropolitan area. They agreed to grow only to a certain size and then to start four or five sister churches in key spots throughout the city. Each church is autonomous, yet it maintains a satellite relationship with the parent church.

3. Reformulation

In many circumstances the better option is neither to resist nor to abandon. Instead, the best plan calls for a *retooling* of present resources. Depending upon the problem, four different elements need to be examined:

a. *Priorities.* If a church is not growing, it may be because it is not focusing upon the right priorities. Priority shifts are needed. Such shifts should result in the establishment of *new units*—both for the adding of new Christians to the church and for the recruiting of more workers—and an increase in *conversion growth.*

For a church to be healthy, it must follow biblical priorities. A priority system was set forth by Christ in John 17:17-23 when He said that His disciples ought to be first committed to Him. After that we read in verse 17, "Sanctify them in truth." Unless members relate to Christ in a growing and Spirit-filled way, the church cannot be healthy. Jesus has called all Christians to become disciples of the Word.

It is interesting to note here that in the New Testament the word "disciple" is used more than 268 times in the Gospels and Acts. It has three basic references. First, it referred to the "professing disciples." These were the curious ones who followed Jesus, as they might follow any teacher of that day. (See John 6:64-66.) Second, there were the "possessing disciples." These were the individuals who learned to trust in Christ and became committed to His teachings. (See John 2:11.) Third, there were "progressing disciples." These were the people who became committed to the truth of what Jesus Christ said and progressed into His likeness through submission. (See John 8:30-32.)

Congregations which set discipleship and witnessing as chief priorities for the church seldom have problems seeing continuous church growth.

b. *Attitudes.* One of the severest hampering elements to a church's growth is a starchy attitude among its people. It is not wrong for a congregation to be firm on its stands on scriptural tenets; however, when a church's routine functions become so rigid and inflexible that they frighten new people away, church growth is then stymied.

Congregations need positive attitudes and open minds. If the church is riveted with negativism, it can never grow. There must be an optimistic mentality and a sense of genuine faith if a church is going to grow. Hebrews 11:1 says that "faith is the assurance of things hoped for, the conviction of things not seen."

We would like to suggest that this type of positive attitude is developed by taking positive approaches in all religious focuses. The pastor and lay leaders must model and then build into the congregation a positive attitude toward God. This could be done by teaching the congregation how to praise. One of the reasons the charismatic churches are growing so rapidly is because they have learned how to praise.

Praise unlocks all sorts of potential in people and churches. It enhances faith in the lives of people. Psalm 34 says, *"I will bless the Lord at all times; His praise shall continually be in my mouth. My soul shall make its boast in the Lord; the humble shall hear it and rejoice. O magnify the Lord with me, and let us exalt His name together."* Note in this passage that the praise has certain qualities about it. First, it is volitional. David said, I *will* praise the Lord. He made it an act of the will. Second, it is continual. We are to bless and praise the Lord *at all times.* David was always praising the Lord. Third, it is individual. The healthy church should be filled with individual praise all the time. Fourth, it's corporate. We are to *exalt His name together,* as a church body. Fifth, it is experiential. God acted when the people praised Him and they were radiant (joyful). They *experienced* the majesty of praise.

In addition to a positive attitude toward God, people need to have a positive attitude about themselves, as expressed through acceptance and belief. This includes the pastor, church lay leaders and all members of the congregation. They must believe it when Psalm 139 says that we were made specially, that we were formed while we were in our mother's womb, not only in our physical substance, but that our basic personalities were also created. We then look at ourselves in the mirror and say, ''Praise God for what He's made me!''

We further need to have a positive view of life. We can best achieve this by offering thanksgiving. In I Thessalonians 5:18, it reads, ''In everything give thanks; for this is God's will for you in Christ Jesus.''

Philippians, Chapter 2, makes it clear that what we are not to do as Christians is to complain or sulk. It says in verses 14 and 15, ''Do all things without grumbling or disputing; that you may prove yourselves to be blameless and innocent, children of God above reproach in the midst of a crooked and perverse generation, among whom you appear as lights in the world.''

It's also important to develop a positive attitude for dealing with problems so that we can rejoice in them. James 1:2-4 says (Phillips' translation), "My brethren, when various trials and tribulations crowd into your lives, don't treat them as intruders but welcome them as friends."

Imagine that: you have problems, you have the flu, your best friend lets you down, someone dies in your family, or perhaps you are under incredible pressure at work, and what are we told to do? Rejoice! We are told not to treat these problems as intruders, but to welcome them as friends. Imagine, embracing them, eagerly? We do this because "the trying of our faith works patience, and we are to let patience have its perfect work in us in order that we might become complete and whole, wanting nothing."

Finally, we need to develop a positive attitude toward other people and express it through affirmation. We should consistently help to lift people. Our thoughts, words and actions ought to be affirming and edifying. We must get rid of all bitterness, anger, resentment, and envy. As Ephesians 4 directs, *"Let no unwholesome word proceed from your mouth, but only such a word as is good for edification . . . Let all bitterness and wrath and anger and clamor and slander be put away along with all malice. Be kind to one another, tenderhearted, forgiving each other, just as God through Christ Jesus also has forgiven you"* (29-32).

We have gone into a great deal of elaboration on attitudes because they are so fundamental to the development of a church. Not only must there be a change in attitude in a technical sense toward priorities and programming, but there also must be a generally healthy attitude toward the various areas of Christian life. After proper attitudes are developed, the sweetness of Christ-centered fellowship becomes a stimulus itself for bringing in new church members.

c. *Property.* For churches with problems, a solution

that is often preferable to moving to a new location is to stay put and attempt to expand the present ministry base. Under this plan adjacent property can sometimes be purchased; worship services can be increased, sometimes to as many as five per Sunday; and classrooms, parking areas, and sanctuaries may be expanded as property and funds become available. Ultimately, however, each congregation must determine its optimum level of ministry. Once this level—whether it is 300 or 3,000—is obtained, resources need to be diverted increasingly toward *extension* and *bridging* strategies.

d. *Expectations.* For churches in the midst of *rural change* the only alternative is to accept more realistic expectations. In villages, where nearly all the residents are church members and where there are no new arrivals, church decline is usually inevitable. Pastors and lay leaders can minister to one another in these isolated settings without the guilt of comparison being imposed upon them. Their problems and needs are unique in American Christianity. However, in less extreme cases, where the unchurched population is small but still existent, expectations can range from moderate decline to moderate growth.

II. PATHWAYS

Several new measures that are helping congregations to plan programs more effectively relate to *growth pathways.* Congregations are learning to conserve and channel their limited energy into ministries of low costs and high fulfillment.

Another term for growth pathways is *people flow;* that is, the means by which unchurched families move toward responsible membership. This flow involves the conversion, restoration, and maturation processes. In the United States the term "people" relates less to tribes,

Figure 6

ALTERNATIVE PEOPLE FLOW DESCRIPTIONS

1. Awareness Stages (Engle 1975:45)

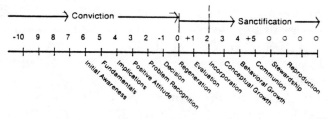

2. Periods of Change (Tippett 1973b:123)

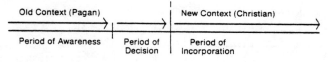

3. Evangelism Levels (Wagner 1971:125-134)

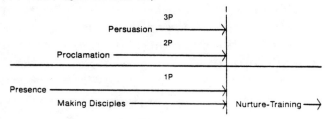

4. Involvement Axis (Wimber 1977:1)

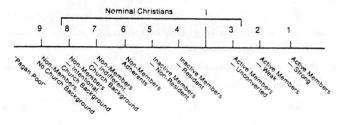

5. Receptivity Axis (Spiritual Distance)
(McGavran 1970:228, Dayton 1978:17)

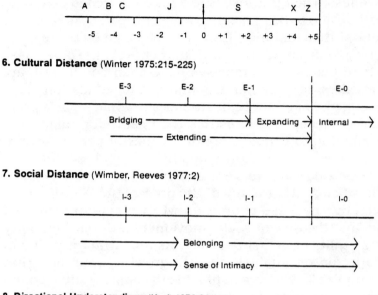

6. Cultural Distance (Winter 1975:215-225)

7. Social Distance (Wimber, Reeves 1977:2)

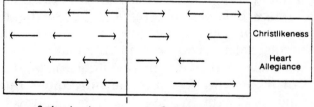

8. Directional Understandings (Kraft 1978:241)

castes, and clans and more to families, lineages, and social classes.

People flow systems provide the framework for goal setting, for strategy preparation, and for measuring effectiveness. Their purpose is to help unchurched people to believe and to belong and to assist Christians in reaching full spiritual maturity. They also shed light on the reasons why people come to a particular church. In some cases where people flow analyses have been conducted, approaches to preaching, calling, and education have changed. For instance, if studies show that a basic problem is loneliness, ministries then can reformulate programming to center more on themes of peace, forgiveness, love, and opportunities for informal fellowship.

People flow analysts are sensitive to persons in *change*. They believe that many of the present strategies are ineffective because church growth workers are working against the flow of social movements. Upward mobility is a reality of present society. As a neutral force, it can work for or against church growth. Churches that recognize its values can provide the appropriate recognition of persons caught in its current—without compromising convictions. Such adjustments illustrate the difference between *upstream* (against the flow) and *downstream* (with the flow) strategies. People-flow strategists also recognize and anticipate *social currents;* they believe that in making evangelistic plans, it is better to move initially *with* the movement rather than against it. For this reason downstream strategies are a common factor in growing churches.

Recognizing upward mobility is not the same thing as approving its effects. Similarly, downstream strategies should not be interpreted as being exclusive or elitist.

Denominational strategies should attempt to reach as many classes and distinct ethnic groups as their resources will permit. For example, with proper plans, mainline denominations could soon begin planting churches along the Mexican border for newly arriving Hispanics. As the constitutencies' social and economic conditions change during the next generation, the new wave of churches would be required to assimilate the new arrivals, who would, in turn, begin their "upward" journey. The simple truth is that more persons can be reached and nurtured in this manner than by approaches that are insensitive to social change. Such forces have previously been criticized as being evil, when, in reality, they provide an opportunity for effective ministry.

ALTERNATIVES

You will note on the graphic designs on pages 68 and 69 that a variety of approaches to people flow definitions has been developed by various researchers.

Engle's chart presents 14 awareness stages and offers a strategy on how to aim church growth. Tippett's scale shows that there are three phases: awareness, followed by a decision, followed eventually by incorporation (membership). Wagner stresses the three keys to evangelism: presence, proclamation and persuasion; this helps planners know what to emphasize. Wimber's scheme of church workers shows where to find the most able church workers.

McGavran's *receptivity axis* is an adaptive tool that helps determine *where to begin* deploying evangelists. It originally contained an alphabetical scheme for isolating peoples according to their *opposition* to Christianity. Those at A, B, or C are extremely antagonistic "leftenders," while those at the "right end" are highly receptive. More recently, the scale has been adapted to numbers ranging from −5 on the left to +5 on the right.

A universal means for assessing *cultural distance* was not available until the appearance of Winter's typology in 1974. It assists leaders in answering the question, *how is strategy designed?* Winter provides the framework for concentrating on internal *evangelism,* as well as *expansion, extension,* and *bridging growth* in settings with an increasing number of cultural barriers.

The Wimber-Reeves' chart helps one determine how to structure programs in order to maximize the social links between individuals and groups. Kraft helps to identify ineffective nurturing and then explains how to correct it.

DESCRIPTION

As has been stated previously, the bottom line of church growth is not determined by the vigor or sincerity with which ministry efforts are conducted, nor the number of decisions being made; instead, it's determined by the number of unchurched persons who are being brought into established congregations. Let's now examine the ways in which people flow analyses can assist this.

a. *Side door and front door discipling.* In the majority of growing churches there is an evangelistic force which virtually draws non-Christians like a magnet through the front door and into the worship service. However, some churches have developed a different philosophy of ministry which calls for meeting non-Christians in the community and bringing them into the church through one of several "side door" activities.

One approach concentrates on a *gospel by attraction;* a second approach focuses on a *gospel by persuasion.* Theologian Johannes Blauw refers to these contrasting forces as centripetal and centrifugal. Centripetal draws people toward the center of a church's activities. This was characteristic of mission activities in the Old Testament. Centrifugal, however, moves people away from the center of activities in an outreach program similar to the church models in the New Testament. Both are means

Figure 7

THE SIDE DOOR INCORPORATION PROCESS

A. The Possibilities

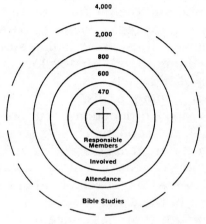

B. The Process

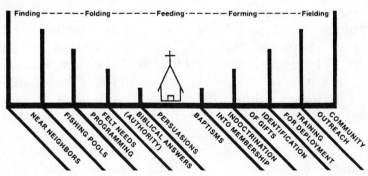

Source: Wimber 1976:1-2

by which lost people can be led to salvation, however.

Front door churches prefer to plan events which will draw non-Christians into the Christian influence. Side door churches have become restless in waiting for the lost to find the way to church. They believe that the message can best be understood in an atmosphere which is non-threatening to the unbelievers. This demands that Christians take the initiative in seeking lost souls on their own home ground and then witnessing to them on the spot. This may call for tent revivals in parks, canvassing door to door in cities, establishing storefront missions in slum neighborhoods, or developing after-hours Christian clubs at high schools.

b. *Front door fishing pools.* Front door American methodologies can be grouped into four primary *fishing pools* (see graph). Each pool represents scores of specific strategies with different labels and target audiences. Each pool contains dozens of hungry "fish." Each type can best be caught with a special kind of bait held at a particular depth in the water.

(1) *Word of mouth* churches concentrate on developing an image of excitement or importance. There are regular articles in the newspapers and notices on billboards about the church's various events. Sometimes it comes about simply by having one neighbor tell another about his pastor or a certain activity in the church which has influenced his life. Other people then become curious enough to want to visit the church. Many non-Christians voluntarily choose to attend a service simply because they've heard from other "satisfied customers."

(2) *High visibility events* are held within the walls of a church and are designed to meet a single need of one homogeneous group of people. Depending upon the circumstances, this might include a speaking appearance by an athlete, a congressman, a psychologist, an entertainer, or any other spokesperson with high credibility

Figure 8

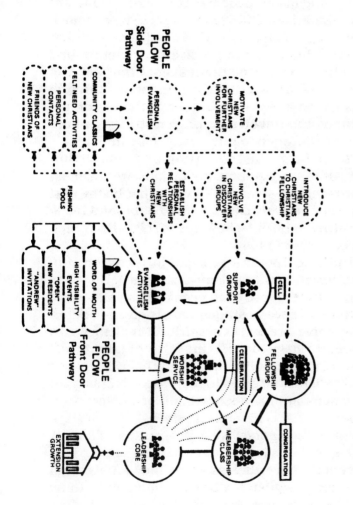

PORTRAIT OF A LARGE MULTI-ENTRY CHURCH

A Composite Model of People Flow in the United States

within a certain target audience.

(3) *"Open" new residents* are new residents who are looking for meaning and purpose, after having broken old ties. Churches that understand this need and respond appropriately bring in new people year round. Usually this involves a combination of introductory letters, telephone calls and personal visits.

(4) *"Andrew" invitations* are given to friends and associates. They can be distinguished from word of mouth contacts by the fact that the guest walks through the front door with a regular member of the congregation. Sometimes this involves a prayer strategy where members are encouraged to pray for specific individuals and pledge to bring at least four people to church during the year. Although personal invitations are the most popular approaches in America, they may not be the best for every church. In many cases, due to habit and tradition, this is the only outreach approach with which church leaders are familiar.

Strategies for incorporating people into church congregations differ from evangelism strategies in that they emphasize *processes* more than *events*. Since assimilation usually follows several stages, care is given to determine where people are in their spiritual maturity and what is needed to help them to move to greater levels of satisfaction and commitment. Often this will involve revising evangelism strategies to increase selectivity for certain audiences and to decrease all-inclusive "shotgun" approaches.

c. *Side door fishing pools.* Many Americans will never enter the front door of a local church except for marriage or funeral services. Nevertheless, these individuals often have sincere needs which can best be ministered to by the Christian message. Growing churches using side door approaches have discovered ways to meet these needs, win a relatively high percentage of these people to Christ, and incorporate them into the fellowship of the Body.

Congregations that "fish" in this manner are classified as *side door churches.* Four primary sources of contacts have been identified, but they represent literally hundreds of specific methods:

(1) *Community classics* are large events held in neutral auditoriums. They are distinguished from high visibility events merely by their location outside the walls of the church. Extensive neighborhood outreach campaigns are included in this category. The local church does not need to be the only vehicle that sponsors and develops these types of events in an outside auditorium. Key individuals in the church could simply open up their homes and invite their friends in for group meetings on a smaller scale. The ministry of Campus Crusade for Christ presently has one focus called the Executive Ministry headed by Col. Nimrod McNair. These individuals specialize in this type of approach. Information about their methods can be picked up by contacting Col. McNair at Executive Ministries, 1924 Clairmont Road, Decator, GA 30033.

(2) *Felt need activities* are smaller in scope than community classics and are designed to meet the isolated needs of certain groups within a single homogenous unit. For one church it might be a motorcycle club for teenagers; for another it might include "potty-training" clinics for young mothers; for a third it might include a diet club for over-eaters. Through these sources the people are led into the church.

Let us take, for instance, a weight counseling clinic for young mothers. Some churches will opt to hold this clinic in the community and will advertise it by putting posters in such places as laundromats, baby stores, and Christian book stores. When the mothers gather for the meeting, they meet other young mothers their same ages who are outstanding, loving, friendly Christians. They greet and welcome them and pick individual women to befriend during the time. One Christian lady who is an authority on weight control presents a program. Toward

Figure 9

COMPOSITE DUAL PATHWAY MODEL

A. Side Door Pathway (Centrifugal)

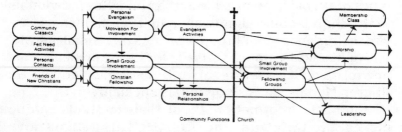

B. Front Door Pathway (Centripetal)

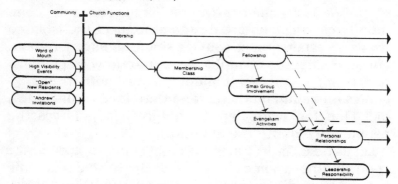

the end, she or another individual says something like, "Well, we've been talking about dieting and physically helping our spirituality today. Let me tell you how the two have helped me better my life." At this point, this person may give a testimony about how she came to know Christ.

Now during this seminar, relationships will build through small group interaction. Some of the Christian mothers will invite the other non-Christians into their homes during the week. They come together initially around a mutual need and in the process form other relationships. This outreach helps bring new people into the body of Christ.

(3) *Personal contacts* are receptive individuals met within the course of a normal week. Lay leaders are trained to sense spiritual needs in others they come in contact with at work, at home, at a shopping center, or at sporting events. Through these relationships lay people have a direct role in leading others to a new life in Christ and fellowship in the local church.

(4) *Friends of new Christians* are often receptive to the witness of a peer who has recently found Christ. When new Christians have been functioning within a local church for more than a year, close ties with non-Christians outside the church tend to disappear. Therefore, some growing churches specialize in training friendly and articulate Christians to meet the friends of new Christians and begin discipling each social sphere out to its fringe.

d. *Side door catching and cleaning.* An old proverb states, "One must *catch* a fish before he can clean it." The same is true about non-Christians: catch them, then cleanse them. Although the exact process varies considerably, five elements of side door discipling can usually be discovered: personal evangelism; motivation for further involvement; establishment of personal relationships; involvement in small group dynamics; and introduction to Christian fellowship.

e. *Side door and front door perfecting.* Side door churches with evidence of steady growth have developed discipling machinery in the community and perfecting machinery in the church. On the other hand, front door churches can disciple and perfect their communities only after non-Christians have entered the worship service. Consequently, their discipling and perfecting objectives are made exclusively among internal activities.

f. *Multiple level commitments.* Growing churches arrange their activities according to several tiers of involvement. In the *worship service* the primary purpose is to strengthen the vertical relationship between God and man. At a second level, fellowship groupings fulfill the human need to belong. At still deeper levels, support and friendship structures undergird a high proportion of members. High levels of congregation satisfaction are repeatedly traced to churches which have more than 40 percent of their members participating in multiple level activities.

g. *A case study in front door perfecting.* A general understanding of what has proved successful in front door church witnessing has been compiled from scores of growing churches. Each of these churches focuses on multiple-level commitments and all see most of their non-Christians won and incorporated into the congregation through one of the four "fishing pools" shown in our chart. One of the best examples currently in operation is the Garden Grove Community Church of Garden Grove, California. Rev. Robert Schuller's main fishing pool is his drive-in parking lot. Each Sunday morning service is a high visibility event in itself, and Schuller's positive, life-changing sermons cause a significant percentage of non-Christians to sign up weekly for the next pastor's class. Rev. Schuller appears several times during each class series, but most of the evangelism and incorporation teaching is delegated to a capable, sensitive associate.

It is in this non-threatening environment that the hook of Christianity surfaces for the first time in the lives of the majority who attend. Each one is skillfully and appropriately established in the faith with solid biblical teaching. All are taught to understand the various internal activities of the church.

After completing the six week pastor's class, about half of the participants become involved in the Sunday school program or some small group activities.

h. *A case study in side door perfecting.* The more than 2,000 member First Baptist Church of Modesto, California, also believes in a multi-focused commitment to the church. However, its 10-year 347 percent rate of growth has been achieved almost exclusively through side door persuasion evangelism. A systematic door-to-door approach is the church's primary fishing pool. Only 15 percent of the non-Christians with whom they share the Gospel initially pray to receive Christ, but half of those in the 15 percent become responsible members of their church. After basic follow-up is completed at both an individual and small group level, the home Bible study becomes the primary tool for Christian education. In 1977, 40 percent of those who actively attended the church completed homework assignments and attended study sessions each week.

i. *A composite multi-entry church.* This variety of church is so named because it has opened numerous doors to the unchurched in response to nearby felt needs. Separate systems of catching and caring respond to the distinctive needs of front door and side door persons. In addition to monitoring the flow of people and activities, church leaders also give attention to the selection and training of new leaders for each activity. They assign priorities to extension growth: new pastoral leaders are chosen and trained; property is acquired; members are prayerfully and financially involved; Christians are multiplied as the number of new units is multiplied.

REFINEMENTS

Understanding several additional factors relating to people flow processes will help you to select specific strategy combinations which are right for your particular church.

a. *Appropriate balance.* Because of the wide range of acceptable ministry options in America, an "ideal" model is virtually useless since no congregation could achieve it. Therefore, the multi-entry concept must remain elastic. In certain cases an effective centripetal approach will produce more growth than can be managed. In other instances almost no growth could be realized by strategies seeking to attract visitors to a central place. After making a determination of the sources for recent growth, churches should begin to broaden their ministry bases gradually by experimenting with several promising strategies in each major category.

A common tendency is to favor just one pathway and to believe that the others are inferior. This is illogical, however. Common sense will tell you that the more approaches you use, the greater the odds will be that you have something that will appeal to everyone. Front door and side door strategies are not synonymous with "come and go" philosophies, "gathering and scattering" or "inside the walls vs. outside the walls" approaches. The multi-entry model presented in this chapter is unique in its identification of the context of the initial contact. Strategies labeled "go" or "scattering" or "outside the wall" are often, in fact, nothing more than front door strategies, since they call for visiting people who have already attended a worship service. Side door audiences are different from front door audiences in that they do not voluntarily attend church. Although their spiritual receptivity may be high, their levels of awareness and commitment to church are often quite low.

b. *Advantages of front door churches.* Congregations

that have generated substantial centripetal forces are able to minister quickly and efficiently. Central operations are easier to manage than those that are decentralized. However, such advantages are sometimes offset by inherent tendencies toward a slower ability to change, a false sense of faithfulness, and an overdependence upon architectural evangelism.

c. *Advantages of side door churches.* In general, centrifugal strategies are more effective in smaller churches where there is greater freedom for adaptability and assertiveness. Not all pastors have been called to lead large front door pulpit ministries. Consequently, larger buildings are not the immediate answer to growth. In only a few cases has the purchase of television equipment proved effective in expanding the worship capacity beyond 2,000. Side door churches are often less formal and less conventional; their language is usually more esoteric and includes more high impact concepts; they have the potential of causing greater alienation between church and community; they perceive themselves as being more counter-cultural and non-mainstream; they are also able to reformulate old meanings and to present them in more relevant ways. In addition, side door churches have the advantage of recruiting the unchurched to a cause or a group, rather than simply to an institution.

The electronic church (television, radio, cassette tape ministries) has surpassed all other side door ministry approaches with respect to modernized outreach efforts. These media also seem to prove the theories about a positive correlation existing between beliefs and church participation. Significantly, recent studies suggest that people are more inclined to join churches after ''believing'' while in non-threatening settings, such as televised services, than they are to ''believe'' after joining churches.

One common danger of side door churches is the tendency to load their initial presentations of the gospel

with too much ethical content. In cases where this occurs members are led to a salvation by works and an acceptance that is overly dependent upon performance.
Side door churches are often criticized, usually unjust-
ly, for their excessive evangelism. In contrast to many
popular theories, evangelism leads to fellowship more
often than fellowship leads to evangelism.

d. *People flow examples.* During the last few years we
have witnessed a rapid increase in the development of
practical people-flow strategies, ranging from conventional approaches (such as busing or television adver-
tisements) to more innovative ideas (including "season
ticket" strategies). What is not often realized, however,
is the amount of preparation and work that is involved
in following through on any particular plan. The "iceberg
principle" states that 10 percent of effective evangelism
time requires 45 percent preparation and 45 percent
preservation. It also takes at least two to three years in
general to design and refine a new evangelistic strategy.
Often churches conclude prematurely that an approach
is just not working. Such judgments are not valid until
an idea has been properly installed and improved upon
for at least a couple of years.

Over the long term it is wise for a congregation not to
limit itself simply to one or two fishing pools. Conditions
can easily change and some pools may soon become
"fished out." Better strategies and greater growth potential can be realized by building a broader-based, more
active, more intentional system. Fortunately, this trend
often develops automatically from effective ministry. As
currents are identified, other ideas and resources tend
to emerge naturally rather than in a manner that is ar-
tificial or contrived. For example, sometimes it is helpful
to distinguish between fishing pools in the community
and incorporation pools in the congregation. Although
both types might be held in homes, they are conducted
for different reasons and for different kinds of persons.

A third group may take on a more assertive style of evangelism. It is in this latter setting, more than any other, that new evangelists are identified and equipped.

When it is time to structure new units, segmenting should be based on relationship ties and other commonalities, rather than on geographic or other arbitrary criteria. Leaders rise to the top quickly in settings where the mixture of enthusiasm is strong and contagious. In front door churches commitment will begin at a low level and increase gradually. Attrition is typically high. In side door churches, demand often begins high and tapers off only slightly during the first few years. The matter of community image also supplies contrasting currents. Front door growing churches generally have a high self image that corresponds to a high image among nearby unchurched residents. On the other hand, the high self image of growing side door churches usually corresponds in a reverse way to the image it projects in the community.

e. *Sodality structures.* A final refinement in dual pathway thinking comes from reflecting upon the movement of Christianity throughout history. Ralph Winter has brought to the attention of the missionary world the fact that God's redemptive purpose has included two complimentary structures. Groups with membership restrictions such as age, sex, or disciplinary standards are termed *sodalities;* those that are non-restrictive and, in principle, desire to include everyone are called *modalities.* In New Testament times the two structures took the form of the synagogue and the missionary band. During the Medieval period they appeared again as the diocese and the monastery. Today, they are seen in the form of parachurch organizations and denominational structures.

Sodalities have caused theological confusion for mission and church scholars alike. Some have proclaimed their illegitimacy, while others have conceded that they are God's permissive will rather than His perfect will.

At the local level sodalities include evangelism teams,

men's clubs and local campus ministries. Unlike these task-oriented evangelistic sodalities, almost anyone can belong to a local church. A study of sodalities is important in the context of people flow because of their structural compatibility with centrifugal strategies. Sodalities are considerably more numerous in first generation side door churches than in well-established front door churches. Their visionary missions into local unchurched spheres often receive prominent recognition by church leaders.

Front door churches are generally less enthusiastic about sodal causes. They are often annoyed by the aggressiveness of sodality leaders and by their persistent exhortation to mobilize members on behalf of their cause. Yet, in studying their role in evangelism, one can make several points in their favor: *first,* their ability to attract the unchurched and to incorporate new Christians is undeniably superior to the ability of modal structures; *second,* although their existence has created tension for churches throughout the ages, they are not an aberration, but a complimentary biblical vehicle for reaching non-Christians; and *third,* possibilities for cooperation with media churches and local para-church sodalities can be explored with a view toward providing *modal* care (traditional church membership) for new converts.

The point is that these para-church organizations ought not to be resented or considered second class. They ought not to be seen as competing, but completing, the work of the body of Christ. God does raise up the local church and the para-church. The two can work well together if both will understand the strengths and weaknesses of the other and allow mutual freedom. If a local church will simply appreciate the work of these para-church organizations by seeking to meet the needs of the leaders, by supporting their work through prayer, finances, and public proclamation, and by helping to develop mutual strategies that will cause the productive evangelism and small group discipleship of these ministries, then God will bless both units in a mighty way. Furthermore, the para-church leaders need to support the local church through prayer and a demonstration of commitment to the leadership of the church. This can be done by giving a portion of their finances to the church, attending the key services and meetings, orally communicating appreciation and by getting involved in a specific ministry in that church.

BLOCKAGE

Harvesting and fishing are fascinating processes to observe. As in most endeavors professionals make the job look easy, whereas amateurs, though often enjoying themselves, lack precision and perspective. The same pattern can be observed in churches. Most common errors made by congregations attempting to establish effective evangelism programs can be grouped according to four categories:

(1) *Process.* Many strategies fail because they emphasize isolated events and programs. In some cases there is too large a gap between decisions and disciples. At other times it may be a single program, such as visitation, that needs to be coordinated with other forms of outreach. Evangelism, reaching out, and receiving new members are not synonymous. Incorporation, believing and uniting are separated and often unrelated activities. Yet, in a particular setting the overall process needs to be clearly understood.

(2) *People.* In some instances the process for church growth is sound, but the workers have not been properly selected and placed. Even with thorough training, certain tasks cannot be carried out effectively. Giftedness is especially important in evangelism. Although everyone can improve in personal witnessing, those chosen to lead

the operation must have intuitive abilities. Without such persons, the authentic message and ministry of a congregation often fails to match the needs of the unchurched. In general, those who witness effectively do so within their own sphere of influence.

Frequently overlooked factors in the selection of people are the use of language, lifestyle, and location. Often neighbors are defined as those within certain geographical boundaries—and especially those next door. In most communities, neighborhoods in the traditional sense no longer exist. Instead, people "neighbor" according to vocational, recreational, and educational commonalities.

(3) *Attitudes.* Even with the right people in the right place using the right process, strategies can fail. Improper attitudes are frequently the cause. There are two varieties—unconscious insensitivity and unintentional exclusiveness. Invisible signs—ones that only visitors see—say "take us or leave us" or simply "keep out." Sometimes a "no" response from a newcomer does not always mean no; however, it may require persistence and creativity before it becomes a "yes." Similarly, expressed reasons for losses among members, including leaders, are not always the real reasons. Some losses are due to irresponsibility.

(4) *Balance.* Some churches are not growing in spite of a healthy flow of persons through the front door and several side doors as well. In such cases the difficulty lies in the size of the "back door"—more people are leaving than are arriving. An equal effort is needed to discover the causes for such departures. Effective strategies require front and side doors that are wide open and back doors that are reserved for legitimate "emergencies" only. Church leaders can assume that unless people become involved in activities other than morning worship, they will not be assimilated permanently.

BEST BOOKS ON PRESCRIPTIONS AND PATHWAYS

The following sources are recommended for further reading on the subjects of overcoming problems and establishing people flow.

1. ADAMS, James Luther
   1966 *Voluntary Associations,* John Knox Press, Richmond.
2. ALTMAN, Irwin and Dalmas A. Taylor
   1973 *Social Penetration: The Development of Interpersonal Relationships,* Holt, Rinehart and Winston, New York.
3. BARCLAY, William
   1975 *Turning to God: A Study of Conversion in the Book of Acts and Today,* Baker, Grand Rapids.
4. ENGEL, James F., Hugh G. Wales, and Martin R. Warshaw
   1975 *Promotional Strategy,* Richard Irwin, Inc., Homewood, Ill.
5. HALDANE, Jean M., Nancy B. Geyer, James C. Fenhagen, James D. Anderson, and J. Barry Evans
   1973 *Prescriptions for Parishes,* Seabury Press, New York.
6. HALL, J.
   1969 *Systems Maintenance: Gatekeeping and the Involvement Process,* Teleometrics, Inc., Monroe, Texas.
7. HESS, Margaret and Bartlett Hess
   1977 *The Power of a Loving Church,* Regal, Glendale.
8. LEWIS, C. Douglass
   1981 *Resolving Church Conflicts,* Harper and Row, New York.
9. POTTER, Burt
   1976 *The Church Reaching Out,* Moore Publishing, Durham, N.C.
10. RAUFF, Edward A.
    1979 *Why People Join the Church,* Pilgrim Press, New York.
11. REED, Millard
    1977 *Let Your Church Grow,* Beacon Hill Press, Kansas City.
12. SCHALLER, Lyle E.
    1978 *Assimilating New Members,* Abingdon, Nashville.
13. SCHALLER, Lyle E.
    1981 *Activating the Passive Church,* Abingdon, Nashville.
14. WAGNER, C. Peter
    1979 *Your Church Can Be Healthy,* Abingdon, Nashville.
15. WINTER, Ralph and R. Pierce Beaver
    1970 *The Warp and the Woof,* William Carey, Pasadena.

CHAPTER FIVE
Understanding Church Typologies

During the final quarter of the twentieth century, the church growth movement will try to flex its muscles in many ways. In its attempts to grow mightier and more coordinated, the church will discover that some of its new "exercises" will work wonderfully, but others will occasionally hamstring the efforts.

As ethnic identity becomes more socially desirable, as minority races increase greatly in numbers, and political splinter groups become more at odds with each other, America will find itself more divided and segmented than ever before. In order to reach out to these various segments of society, while losing its mission and testimony, the church will have to develop well-defined ministry strategies.

Yet understanding the advantages and limitations of a particular strategy in a specific situation will continue to be one of the most crucial aspects of developing a good plan for church growth. One of the chief reasons most churches don't grow is that they are using the wrong game plan.

Many times a strategy for growth looks logical on paper, yet later proves to be disastrous in practice. Why? Usually it's because church leaders have tried to put square pegs into round holes: they've put a system into practice before considering if their particular church lends itself well to that system.

Evidences of such mismatchings can be seen routinely. A fundamentalist congregation builds its church in a strong Roman Catholic neighborhood and soon finds itself faltering. A physically small church expands its membership rolls before its new facilities are ready, and winds up overloading and crushing itself. A metropolitan church moves to the suburbs to have more space, and suddenly discovers its city-dwelling members are resigning because they don't want to drive the distance. In each instance the strategy for growth proved incorrect.

Among the most challenging tasks confronting church growth efforts in this country today is the need to establish a system of useful church *typologies* (the specific characteristics of each church). The need for such a system is as timely as it is fundamental. To be effective, ministers must understand and accept the kind of church in which they minister—and be able to explain the nature of their church to both members and colleagues.

One way to describe a church is to list its denominational affiliation, such as the Baptist Church or the Lutheran Church, or by such theological images as the sacramental fellowship, the house of God or the Body of Christ. While these descriptive terms are true, there are more useful ways to categorize congregations. Developing these categories is important to those interested in church growth because they reveal "common ground" among the various denominations and the numerous independent churches. This helps to unite Christians, as well as slow down the splintering of social groups. Let's look now at how categories and church types are best identified in relationship to church growth.

IDENTIFICATION PROCESSES

The social sciences during the last two decades have shown a dramatic increase in their use of models and paradigms. The term *paradigm* (meaning an organized

Figure 10

CONTEMPORARY TYPOLOGIES WITH AUTHORS

Historical

Age (Schaller)

**Growth
Rates** (Wagner)

Contextual

Regional (composite)

**Urban-
Rural** (Jones)

Image (Walrath)

Institutional

1. **Beliefs**

   Philosophical Style
   (Dulles, Baumann)

   Ecclesiastical-Historical
   (composite)

2. **Composition**

   Heritage (composite)

   Creativity (Wimber)

   Progressiveness (Wimber)

3. **Leadership**

   Operational Style
   (Grier, Burns)

4. **Structure**

   Polity (Jewett)

   Size (Schaller)

   Architecture (Snyder)

   People Flow (Reeves)

5. **Health**

   Pathology (Wagner)

unified group, such as a denomination) has received wide usage since the publication of Thomas Kuhn's influential book, *The Structure of Scientific Revolutions* (1962). In analyzing one of his paradigms, Kuhn says that most people see the world through a specific set of "spectacles" (opinions), and problems viewed through these spectacles have more clear-cut yes or no answers.

Kuhn also says that a person can fully share the outlook of only one tradition at a time. In other words, someone who is a member of a particular religious sect or congregation has accepted certain ideas which, when combined, make up the overall *belief* of that religious group. This person adopts assumptions and expectations which are in accordance with that religious group's beliefs, and he or she interprets experiences according to the group's traditions and religious stances.

Such stances, attitudes, and traditions are often spoken of as *worldview*, though this latter term is usually considered to be more of a "total" view of reality than a paradigm or a specific example.

When a person's worldview shows that he or she is following a variety of different beliefs, that person is not a full member of any single coherent church or religious tradition. In short, that person is confused, still searching for answers and quite at odds with all traditional religious groups.

Now, common sense tells us that even in an established church there are going to be many people who will not be in precise agreement with each other on every point found in the New Testament. That's fine. Biblical study and analysis should be encouraged in all churches. If the members of a particular church are in basic agreement on the key elements (such as salvation, baptism, and the Bible), they can still be of the same sect or denomination or congregation.

Julienne Ford suggests a concept of interrelated paradigms (patterns) as consisting of "thoughts wrapped up in thoughts about thoughts" (*Paradigms and Fairy Tales,* 1975:2, 37-39). For her, these "linked paradigms of thought" serve as patterns both for the gaining of knowledge and for the knowledge itself.

The analysis that follows will reflect an understanding of the Bible and of history that includes a considerable range of inspired and overlapping paradigms:

When two people from very different backgrounds encounter each other, they begin to "rub off" on each other. Both observe and learn from the other. They modify. After awhile, neither is the same as he or she was before. This move to common viewpoints leads to a *paradigm shift.*

And just as two people can modify each other, so can two congregations. When people from one congregation are exposed to the radio broadcasts, televised sermons, religious magazines and books produced by another congregation, and vice versa, a paradigm shift occurs in congregations. Very few congregations are isolated from contradictory influences. Thus, if a congregation wishes both to grow in numbers and to hold fast to its established doctrines, it is going to have to figure out how to keep its present members from being swayed by outside influences.

PARADIGMS AND TAXONOMIES

The paradigm concept has several advantages over the more traditional means of comparing various church groups. When properly comprehended, paradigmatic viewpoints tend to converge from formerly "objective" or "subjective" extremes toward a more balanced "in between" range. Such a perspective also helps to avoid the perils of reductionism, in which religion is taken to be entirely the product of psychological or sociological forces.

Another benefit to understanding the nature of paradigms is for the participants themselves. Tremen-

Figure 11

A TENTATIVE TAXONOMY OF CHURCH TYPES*

A. Historical (Development)

1. **Beginning** (4)
2. Pastoral Tenures
3. Staff Progression (3)
4. Facilities Progression (3)
5. **Growth Rates** (4)
6. Migration Pattern (2)
7. Assimilation Pattern
8. Crises
9. Denominational Loyalty

B. Contextual (Local, external)

1. **Region**
2. **Rural, Urban**
3. Community Composition
4. Change (2)
5. Receptivity (3)
6. Range
7. **Image** (2)

C. Institutional (Internal)

1. **Beliefs**
   a. **Theology**
   b. Purpose
   c. **Philosophy**
   d. Intensity
   e. Corporate Image
   f. Satisfaction
   g. Expectations
   h. Growth Importance
2. **Composition**
   a. **Heritage** (2)
   b. Education
   c. Vocations
   d. Income

   e. Expressed Values
   f. Lifestyle Manifestations
   g. **Creativity**
   h. **Progressiveness**
   i. Age & Sex
3. **Leadership**
   a. Education
   b. Experience
   c. Family (4)
   d. **Style** (3)
   e. Gifts
   f. Compatability
4. **Structure**

   a. **Polity**
   b. **Size** (3)
   c. Staff (3)
   d. Workers (2)
   e. Program (3)
   f. **People Flow** (2)
   g. **Facilities** (3)
   h. Planning (3)
   i. Financial (2)
5. **Health**
   a. **Pathology**
   b. Potential

dous achievements have resulted from the high level commitments and determined tenacity which often accompany membership within a particular research paradigm. The key is to maintain the delicate tension between a high commitment to a personal paradigm, and high tolerance and respect for those of differing paradigms.

Admittedly, this is not an easy balance to strike. Most people are eager to endorse and support self-interest aims. However, when rational thought can replace personal desires and when fairness can supercede cultural prejudice, church units can be linked successfully.

The above matter is not unrelated to a crisis which occurred during the 1970s in every discipline from philosophy and theology to social theory. It centers on the fact that cherished concepts such as "knowledge," "theory," "practice," even "reality" and "non-reality" (concepts we have long grown accustomed to as vehicles for understanding ourselves and our world) showed serious signs of cracking and splitting. They no longer were as stable as they once seemed. Part of this perplexing trend could be attributed to the erosion of long-standing paradigms (the established institutions and practices of previous eras, that is).

It should be emphasized that the process of paradigm or institution building is considerably more complex in the social sciences than it is in the physical sciences. Therefore, it is often difficult to find one set of specific factors that adequately accounts for why things can change so greatly and so rapidly.

As a rule, paradigms—particularly religious denominations—do not suddenly come into existence at a specific time; nor are they the result of a conscious effort to move a group of people toward an end goal by a given date. They are, instead, the overall result of a variety of complex developments which blend together over a long period of time by a sizable number of people.

The obvious development of numerous overlapping macro-systems during the twentieth century can be attributed to the widespread expansion of knowledge. This new wealth of information is the result of two things: incredible technological advances and a record number of people devoting themselves to advanced research. The effect has been a serious re-evaluation of previously held values and conceptions.[1]

In the realm of theology, these re-evaluations have been most noticeable in the way church scholars and church members have begun to recognize the diverse ways in which Scripture has historically been viewed. There is, naturally, a basic understanding that people will try to form their own interpretations of biblical concepts, such as how the Church should be organized. On the other hand, however, even many conservative scholars are now no longer insisting that there is only one scriptural interpretation of inspired writings; they have begun to accept a variety of plausible interpretations and explanations of biblical passages.

The central issue in the matter is how to determine the basis of ecclesiology. How much tolerance should be allowed for *functional* definitions as opposed to *ontological* descriptions? How much is the preaching of the Word and how much the administration of the sacraments? How much is *visible* and how much is *invisible?* How much is *temple* or *body* or *family?* The questions do not lead to responses. They reveal substantial limitations in present definitions and at the same time show enormous gaps in interdisciplinary research.

Such complex images also confront the difficulty of *theological verification.* When dedication and empirical tests are ruled out, all that is left is a general "discernment of spirits." In discussing the potential consequences of destructive paradigm shifts (denominational clashes) which could cause polarization, incomprehension, and discouragement, Avery Dulles concludes:

Whatever may be said of the relative merits of the various paradigms one must recognize that the transition from one to another is fraught with difficulties. Each paradigm brings with it its own set of images, its own rhetoric, its own values, certitude, commitments and priorities. It even brings with it a particular set of preferred problems. When paradigms shift, people suddenly find the ground cut out from under their feet . . . Theologians, who ought to be able to shift their thinking from one key to another, often resist new paradigms because these eliminate problems on which they have built up a considerable expertise, and introduce other problems with regard to which they have no special competence (1974:35, 19-36).

In addition to overlap, reduction, and rigidity, there are limitations due to the *blending of definitions* between sects and denominations. New and varied views on matters such as evangelism, renewal, growth, and charismatic expression all have an influence on changing the previous images. New urban patterns also result in the emergence of other non-traditional church types. Fluidity can be observed similarly in the *varying components* and *criteria* that determine new church types. Jones lists six criteria: location, image, new members, concept of community, social ties and size (1976:36-37). Ryals prefers a different mix of five: community, meeting place, membership, forms of ministry and leaders (1979:94-106).

The difficulties can also be found at the opposite extreme, in the search for *boundaries.* For example, one might ask whether the new variables we mentioned might force a person to abandon all previously held claims to truth. Fortunately, most people today are nowhere near that naive. But this hasn't always been the case. For example, during the 1930s a man named William Hocking suggested that Christians should just stop preaching *any* kind of doctrine for awhile and, instead, should just become very busy with providing material aid to needy people. During this period, the ecumenical movement worked so hard at becoming helpful, it eventually became nothing more than "a seminar on social theology and comparative ecclesiology" (Rouse and Neill 1967:573). Its only criteria for evaluating theology were tolerance and expansion of the kingdom. Even today such denominations as the Friends' Church (Quakers), the Church of the Brethren, and some Mennonites still hold fast to these same criteria.

A final difficulty in classifying types of churches is a tension between those who demand technical accuracy and those who are more concerned with being practical. Systems that are overly rigid and strict are usually difficult to put into general use. Overlapping descriptions cannot always be arranged in a neat row or placed within a multi-dimensional diagram. Life isn't that simple and neither is worship.

There doesn't appear to be any limit to the number of ways in which churches can be perceived. Some classifications are more useful in certain instances than in others. Until more refinement has taken place and a consensus concerning importance has been reached, elaborate schemes will have very little usefulness. In some cases, due to excessive detail, they might even become counterproductive, by turning persons against the use of all typologies.[2]

Several suggestions can help to overcome any frustrations in the use of typologies. *First,* it is important to recognize that each "type" has its own range of *appropriateness.* Personal preferences and contextual factors must both be considered when selecting types. *Second,* all types are further limited by man's inability to comprehend the mysteries of God. As divine realities, churches will never be fully understood. Prudence demands, therefore, that we should avoid tendencies toward overstatement and universal application. *Third,* in the planning process typologies should be given careful consideration during the early phases, and especially during steps two through five and seven (see graphs). When included in the context of designing new strategies, plans can be made more quickly and with greater certainty of success. greater certainty of success.

Typologies are nothing more than classifications. They help us understand other churches, other Christians, and other doctrinal stances. Without such knowledge, we cannot help our own churches remain strong in their beliefs nor reach out to the lost who have no beliefs at all.

Footnotes for Chapter 5

1. For other contributions to paradigm analyses see Eister (1974), Denisoff, Callahan, and Levine (1975), Eisenstadt and Curelaru (1976), Grant (1977), McIntire (1977), Laborit (1977), Schelling (1978), and Kee (1980).

2. One of the complex issues in this regard is the degree to which *taxonic domain theories* can apply to the classification of churches. *Generic* types—those having wide general application—will in the long run prove to be more valuable than those that are obscure with highly technical distinctions (Clinton 1980:11-14).

Best Books on Contemporary Typologies

The following 15 books have been selected to represent the major types of churches discussed in Chapter 5.

1. ARMSTRONG, Ben
    1979   *The Electric Church,* T. Nelson, Nashville.
2. BARBOUR, Ian G.
    1974   *Myths, Models and Paradigms: A Comparative Study in Science and Religion,* Harper and Row, New York.
3. BAUMANN, Dan
    1976   *All Originality Makes a Dull Church,* Vision House, Santa Ana.
4. DRIGGERS, B. Carlisle, ed.
    1979   *Models of Metropolitan Ministry,* Broadman Press, Nashville.
5. DUDLEY, Carl S.
    1979   *Making the Small Church Effective,* Abingdon, Nashville.
6. DULLES, Avery
    1974   *Models of the Church,* Doubleday, Garden City.
7. HEFLEY, James C.
    1977   *Unique Evangelical Churches,* Word, Waco.

  8. KRAFT, Charles H.
      1979   *Christianity in Culture: A Study in Dynamic Theologizing
             in Cross-Cultural Perspective*, Orbis, Maryknoll.
  9. MARTIN, Ralph P.
      1980   *The Family and the Fellowship: New Testament Images
             of the Church*, Eerdmans, Grand Rapids.
 10. NOYCE, Gaylord
      1973   *Survival and Mission for the City Church*, Westminster,
             Philadelphia.
 11. SCHALLER, Lyle E.
      1975   *Hey, That's Our Church!*, Abingdon, Nashville.
      1980   *The Multiple Staff and the Larger Church*, Abingdon,
             Nashville.
 12. SNYDER, Howard A.
      1976   *The Problem of Wine Skins: Church Structure in a Techno-
             logical Age*, Inter-Varsity, Downers Grove.
 13. SPITTLER, Russell P., ed.
      1976   *Perspectives on the New Pentecostalism*, Baker Book
             House, Grand Rapids.
 14. ZUNKEL, C. Wayne
      1982   *Growing the Small Church: A Guide for Church Leaders*.
             David C. Cook, Elgin, Illinois.

CHAPTER SIX
Historical and Contextual Typologies

As noted in the graphs and illustrations in the previous chapter, there are 21 basic categories of church types. Prior to 1980, however, there were fewer than a dozen. This shows a new momentum for not only reclassifying church types from *historical, contextual* and *institutional* views, but also from new perspectives and typologies.

Such supplemental classifying is necessary in order to better understand each particular church's growth needs and growth opportunities. Matching the proper church growth plan with the right church can only be done when the planner has a complete grasp of the *type* of church being helped. In this chapter we will help to create a variety of "handles" by which a planner can take hold of a church and help it to grow. The process begins, naturally, with properly analyzing and classifying the church.

HISTORICAL TYPOLOGY

Churches may be classified by age much the same way people are. Let's review the varied stages of a church's life.

Infant churches are newly established congregations up to three years of age. They are usually small in membership and may or may not have their own facilities. Their style and composition is greatly determined by the nature of their parental link. Some new churches are carefully planned, whereas others happen quite spontaneously. Very few have more than a basic level of programming and policies. Usually, new congregations fall into these six categories: mission; minority; style-centered; redeveloped area; traditional suburban; or ecumenical.[1]

Childhood churches range from 3 to 12 years in age and concentrate on defining themselves more carefully by experimenting with several different approaches to worship and management for themselves and their communities. These are often years of rapid growth mixed with sporadic tensions. Much of the planning is done by trial and error. It is rare for churches to have several staff workers before the end of this childhood phase.

Adolescent churches range from 15 to 20 years in age and usually lack a distinctive image in the community. They often have not reached full institutional strength. Besides the community "identity crisis," there also can develop some tension between the pioneers (those who established the church) and the homesteaders (those who have joined during the last five years). Enthusiasm for new programs frequently decreases during this period and, consequently, most adolescent churches absorb considerably less than half of the prospective members who visit them on Sunday morning. There is also a tendency to oversell what is perceived by more experienced outsiders as a rather limited and unoriginal program.

Young adult churches are from 20 to 40 years old. They often experience at least one plateau period of no new growth during this phase; some never recover. One of the major causes is the turnover of several pastors and/or assistant pastors, frequently accompanied by an increased tension between homesteaders and pioneers. A false sense of security may develop after paying off the mortgage and expanding worship hours to two services.

Very few congregations realize that their annual rate of growth has been dropping steadily and that an increasing proportion of their budget is being allocated each year to maintenance rather than innovation. Many churches shift during this phase from a shotgun programming approach, in which they try many different things, to the rifle approach, which limits them to using only two or three combinations that have seemed to work best. The shift from first to second generation is as significant as any change that congregations experience.[2]

Middle-age churches, from 40 to 60 years, are almost always plateaued or declining in membership due to several subtle or predictable changes that occurred during their previous two decades. Often the community will have changed in ethnic composition or population. In the case of rural churches, the population has been moving away at the rate of as much as three to seven percent per year. A combination of these circumstances frequently results in an elevation of the average age of members beyond the critical level of 50 years. Once this occurs it is highly unlikely that the church will recover to its previous form.

Historic churches have existed for at least two full generations and are often listed among the community landmarks by the Chamber of Commerce. Their growth pattern is typically plateaued with a gradual replacement of departing members by new arrivals who have an appreciation for history and ornamental liturgy. In the rare cases of growing middle-age or historic churches, one usually discovers a dynamic leader who has been pastoring the congregation for the past five to ten years, or one discovers that a new kind of membership has gradually become the dominant voice. Such churches, therefore, have experienced either a spiritual renewal or a sociological transfusion.

These chronological ages of churches help the church growth enthusiast to know the general natures and behavior patterns of churches at various periods of their existence. But, there are more specific ways to analyze a church from an historic viewpoint.

Consider these factors, for example:

> –*Pastoral Tenure*—How many pastors has the church had and how long did each stay?
>
> –*Facilities Development*—When and how were the physical facilities of the church upgraded and what consequent effect did this have on church attendance and membership?
>
> –*Migration Patterns*—How much incentive is there in the church's community for new generations to remain in town? What factors of community development have led to an influx of new people?
>
> –*Crises*—Have any church, community, or regional conflicts or abrupt changes resulted in a subsequent alteration in church procedures or church growth?
>
> –*Denominational Loyalty*—Has the local church had any conflicts with the denomination it allies itself with and, if so, has this led to a lack of national support for the local unit?

Studying church types from an historical perspective helps the advocate of church growth in several ways: (1) it enables him or her to know which long established patterns in a church should be re-examined; (2) it explains why a church's growth pattern may have had severe dips or frequent plateaus; (3) it helps to establish where a church should be in its overall growth process; and (4) it helps one to anticipate which problems may arise at each phase of church aging.

GEOGRAPHICAL TYPOLOGY

Enlightening characteristics of churches can be obtained by studying contextual distinctions, such as qualities related to region, urban-rural orientation, and image. In this overview, cultural variations are given for major geographical divisions only.[3]

New England churches, located in Connecticut, Maine, Massachusetts, New Hampshire, Rhode Island, and Vermont, come in two varieties: those north of the Boston and Syracuse-Albany metropolitan belts and those that are within these two densely populated urban areas. Together, they comprise what is known as a "Yankee" value system—a combination of frugality, conservatism, and inventiveness. Personal income in this area exceeds the national average by 10 percent and more than 50 percent of the church members in most New England counties are Roman Catholic. Only two counties contain as much as 25 to 50 percent Methodist congregations; and most of these churches represent the more liberal wing of Methodists. Population and church membership are increasing only slightly each year, and, with the exception of the extreme west, there are more unchurched persons here per capita than in any part of the country.

Mid-Atlantic churches in New Jersey, New York, and Pennsylvania, contain a disproportionate number of persons working in the manufacturing industries (32 percent). In contrast, only two percent of the working population are farmers. Churches are growing slightly faster here than in New England, but there are high concentrations of unchurched populations, especially in the non-industrial sections. Methodists and Lutherans are considerably stronger in this region than in New England, but most of the counties have a solid majority of Roman Catholic church members.

Midwest churches are fairly evenly distributed throughout the states of Illinois, Indiana, Iowa, Kansas, Michigan, Minnesota, Missouri, Nebraska, North Dakota, Ohio, South Dakota, and Wisconsin. There is more variety in this region due to the fact that Methodists, Lutherans, Catholics, and Baptists are fairly evenly represented. Approximately 75 percent are urban churches and 25 percent rural churches. There are more churches per capita among these states than in any region except the Deep South. Most urban counties have a moderate growth potential, and there are certain pockets of extremely receptive peoples. Other counties have an exceptionally low potential for new churches due to the high annual rates of "out-migration."

Pacific Coast churches in California, Oregon, and Washington, minister to a population that is 90 percent urban. Four-fifths of the churches (as well as the unchurched) are in California. This region contains both the fastest growing churches in the country and the counties with the highest percentage of unchurched populations. Although there are more Catholics than Protestants in the West, the Protestants are more visible, more vocal, and come in more varieties here than in any part of the nation. The highest immigration rates, both foreign and within the United States, are in this region, where there are also as many ethnic churches as in the entire rest of the country. Perhaps the highest untapped potential for new churches is among the Hispanic peoples of Southern California.

Rocky Mountain churches (Colorado, Montana, Nevada, Idaho, Utah, and Wyoming) are evenly dispersed among a population that is 50 percent rural and 50 percent urban. There are four internal areas which are dominated by Catholic, Lutheran, Mormon and Methodist churches, respectively. Growth potential is moderate to good in most counties, with the exception of Utah and the rural sections of Idaho and Montana.

Southern churches are predominately baptistic in theology and are evenly distributed throughout Alabama, Arkansas, Delaware, Florida, Georgia, Kentucky, Louisiana, Maryland, Mississippi, North Carolina, South Carolina, Tennessee, Virginia, and West Virginia. These churches have moderate to good growth potential in spite of the fact that there are fewer unchurched people here than in any part of the country. Fewer than half of the churches are non-Baptist and almost one-third of them are ethnically more than 90 percent "Black." "White" churches have a high percentage of members whose origins can be traced to England, Ireland or Scotland. There also is a greater commonality of style in southern churches than in other regions. Church expansion is largely the result of centripetal structures, with great emphasis upon revivalistic services.

Southwestern churches (Arizona, New Mexico, Oklahoma, Texas) can be grouped according to three distinct cultures: Indian, Spanish, and Anglo-American. Some counties, particularly in Arizona, have excellent growth potential, whereas others (notably in the rural parts of Oklahoma and Texas) have relatively low potential. The region tends to be divided denominationally between Catholics in the west and Baptists in the east.

URBAN/RURAL TYPOLOGY

The placement of a church within, near, or far away from a city can have a major impact on its growth potential, its variety of congregational members, and the financial support it can expect for efforts at church growth. Although a variety of labels have been developed by more than a dozen research analysts for the various geographical boundaries in and around a city, they can effectively be summarized by the five areas we are about to examine.[4] (The graph outline found in this chapter will also provide you with a detailed overview.)

Downtown churches can be found at the core of large metropolitan areas. They come in three varieties: *midtown, inner-city,* and *inner-urban*. (1) *Mid-town churches* are within the commercial centers of large metropolitan areas, among banks, governmental offices, and large department stores. Even though most residents do not actualy reside downtown, they consider it home because it meets their needs for work, entertainment, or retail goods and services. Mid-town churches are usually the largest and most established of their denominations. Their constituency is broad ranged socially and economically, and the church's programming is diverse enough to meet all needs.

(2) *Inner-city churches* can be found amidst run-down housing and areas plagued by high crime rates and serious social problems. These congregations are usually fewer than 300 people in size. Programming often emphasizes drug rehabilitation, self-defense, career training, and counseling. Each ministry is predominantly among a single ethnic group from the lower economic level. The general style is relational, practical, and liberal.

(3) *Inner-urban neighborhood churches* are located in areas adjacent to the heart of the city, near a variety of small businesses, duplexes, and multiple-story apartments. Residents are ethnically mixed and range from lower-middle to middle economic levels. Churches vary considerably in composition and style, but usually are fewer than 300 people in size, with slow to moderate growth at best.

Metro-regional (outer urban) churches are most frequently found at the edge of the urban population, next to the intersection of two or more major traffic arteries. Members drive further than normal to attend services and non-members are made aware of the location because of extensive advertising. This kind of church is usually large in size with a heavy concentration of white middle to upper-middle class families living in single unit dwellings.

Suburb churches, sometimes referred to synonymously as *neighborhood churches,* come in at least five varieties. In a strict sense, *neighborhood* churches can be distinguished from all others by their limited drawing range. Members typically drive short distances and only rarely are persons attracted from other parts of the city.

(1) *City suburb churches* are within townships of more than 50,000 residents, and are usually more than a 20-minute drive from the commercial district. They have a distinctive community identity and their membership has a high percentage of city commuters, including professionals and executives. These churches can be found in every range of size, style, and ethnic composition. They also represent every conceivable pattern of growth.

(2) *Metropolitan suburb churches* are located in residential communities between the more established city suburbs. Both the towns and churches have been built since 1950, and although the residents are well-supplied with local services, they do not have a clear historical identity. Church members are mostly middle to upper-middle class, with very few ethnic groups represented, and the majority of members drive fewer than three miles to attend services. Traffic generally flows not toward but perpendicular to the city center.

(3) *Fringe suburb churches* are invariably under 10 years old, because their communities have only been recently established to meet the needs of a young, affluent and mobile population which is seeking to escape the pressures of life in the city. Growth rates of churches usually correspond to the growth rate of the community itself. Members come almost exclusively from within the township and usually subscribe to the community values of privacy, strict commercial zoning and abundant recreation.

(4) *Fringe village churches* are distinct from fringe suburb churches in that they are located slightly further away from the commercial center and have evolved from an original independent rural settlement. Residents, therefore, are of two basic types: the older long-term residents and the younger recently-arrived families seeking a quiet village atmosphere. The newer churches grow steadily as they attract recent arrivals, whereas the more established churches are invariably plateaued or declining.

Figure 12

URBAN-RURAL CHURCH TYPOLOGIES

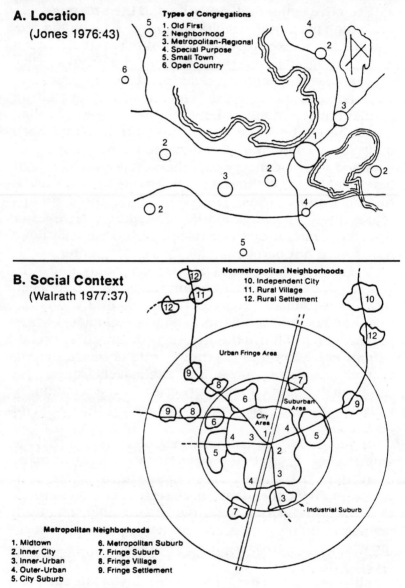

A. Location
(Jones 1976:43)

Types of Congregations
1. Old First
2. Neighborhood
3. Metropolitan-Regional
4. Special Purpose
5. Small Town
6. Open Country

B. Social Context
(Walrath 1977:37)

Nonmetropolitan Neighborhoods
10. Independent City
11. Rural Village
12. Rural Settlement

Urban Fringe Area

Suburban Area

City Area

Industrial Suburb

Metropolitan Neighborhoods

1. Midtown   6. Metropolitan Suburb
2. Inner City   7. Fringe Suburb
3. Inner-Urban   8. Fringe Village
4. Outer-Urban   9. Fringe Settlement
5. City Suburb

(5) *Fringe settlement churches* are located even further from the city's center and contain a more diverse mixture of residents due to poor and often non-regulated zoning practices. New churches are rarely located in these areas. Usually only one or two small churches have been established; the bulk of their membership comes from the agriculturally related occupations and non-suburban homes. A very low percentage of people attend from mobile homes or from the newly built customized homes on plots of from one to three acres.

Independent city, or *small town churches,* can be found in towns of 5,000 to 30,000 people completely isolated from the direct influence of metropolitan cities. Membership totals are often declining due to an employment crisis at the major manufacturing company. Although small churches from several of the major denominations can be found in this region, there almost never is more than one church from any particular denomination. Congregations, therefore, must serve a broad constituency and, hence, are often located near the commercial core.

Country churches come in two types, both of which function normally as a place of worship, a church school, and occasionally as a special activity center.

(1) *Rural village churches* are invariably small and often share a pastor with another village. Their members are mostly related to the agricultural occupations and often travel as much as 30 miles to attend services in the commercial and social center.

(2) *Rural settlement churches* are the only church in a five to 50 mile radius. They are frequently located beside the only store and gas station which may or may not still be in business, dependent upon its proximity to the interstate highway system and the competition from neighboring villages. Members attend from the cluster of houses surrounding the church or from farms within 10 to 20 miles.

COMMUNITY IMAGE TYPOLOGY

Churches can also be defined by their social posture vis-a-vis the surrounding community. Visitation patterns and image have a high correlation for the following three types:

Dominant, or *prestige churches* are usually among the largest churches in a particular area and are often located in the downtown district. A high percentage of a city's elite and powerful citizens worship in this type of church. The churches' architectural designs are invariably the best in their specific sections of the country. These churches are perceived by the community and by other churches in the area as the most influential churches.

Subordinate, or *secondary churches* are the "others" that live in the shadow of nearby prestige churches, usually from the same denomination. They are often overlooked because of their inconspicuous location and are usually dependent upon the dominant churches to model effective ministry programs.

Exclusive churches are counter-cultural in beliefs and lifestyle and do not therefore compete with the dominant or subordinate types. They are often theologically conservative, with strict membership requirements and rigid convictions concerning proper Christian practices.

SUMMARY

Historical and contextual typologies help a church growth analyst place his or her church in its proper place in regard to community and religious identities. The more one knows about a church's problems and potential, the more effectively one is able to develop its growth strategy.

Footnotes for Chapter 6

1. Jones (1976:19-24).
2. For other descriptions of such transformations see Nida (1960:7), Moberg (1962:118-125), Kelley (1972:103-4), Kraft (1977:594), Hefley (1977:107-130), and Dudley (1979:33-42).
3. Unfortunately, no uniform manner of describing U.S. cultural regions has emerged. Most analyses range from 6 to 28 geographical types. See, for example, Gastil (1975) and the Population Reference Bureau Bulletin, (vol. 31, October 1976). For a fascinating travel guide to America's religious background according to eight regions, see Vuillemier and Vuillemier (1976).
4. The major sources, in chronological order are: Belew (1971:80-141), *country* and *small town, suburban* and *downtown;* Schaller (1975:55-77), *ex-neighborhood* and *ex-rural;* Jones (1974) and (1976:39-43), *old first, neighborhood, metropolitan-regional, small town* and *open country.*

SUGGESTED READING LIST

The same books referred to in Chapter Five will also cover material found in Chapter Six.

CHAPTER SEVEN
Institutional and Unofficial Typologies

We have seen that the age and location of a church can have a great deal to do with its potential for growth. Whereas these physical factors are extremely important to consider, they certainly are secondary when compared to such *institutional typologies* as beliefs, composition, leadership, structure and policy. We will now turn our attention to these institutional elements to see how they create an impact on church growth.

I. INSTITUTIONAL TYPOLOGIES

BELIEFS

Of all the institutional typologies more has been written about beliefs than any other. Beliefs can, in turn, be broken down into descriptions concerning *theology, purpose, philosophy, intensity, corporate image, satisfaction, expectations,* and *growth importance.* However, existing classifications fall into two categories only: *philosophy* and *theology.*

A. *Philosophy typologies* are sometimes referred to as *style typologies.* They reflect the unique differences in the way ministry is performed on the local level. At least nine different styles have been observed. We will briefly outline and summarize these nine styles.

Soul-winning churches emphasize the primary importance of evangelism. All other purposes for their existence are subordinate to bringing salvation to the lost. Sunday morning sermons focus on non-believers, and the role of Christians as evangelists is emphasized regularly from the pulpit and reinforced by the leadership at other church functions. Though often criticized for oversimplifying salvation, for those who subscribe to this style, the transformation is both profound and permanent.

Classroom churches emphasize the primary importance of knowing God's Word. Sermons generally consist of at least 40 minutes of expository preaching on Sunday morning and a similar amount on Sunday evening, and usually at a mid-week service as well. Members are eager to learn and often take notes at each service. Those who throng to classroom churches claim that it results in a deeper understanding of God and an increased desire to serve Him.

Life situation churches de-emphasize instructional learning and concentrate on meeting the needs of individuals. Sermons are relationally-oriented and there is a strong sense of one's responsibility within the Christian body. Sharing, prayer, and discussion replace formal classroom teaching, and leaders stress the importance of meeting and accepting people for what they *are* rather than talking to them in regard to what they *ought* to be. Although such *community* or *fellowship* models can lead to interdependence, alienation, and false expectations, close relationships and discovery learning—with an elastic approach to hermenuetics—can, in fact, attract and hold people who otherwise reject more static models.

Social action churches, also termed *diaconal churches,* emphasize the importance of loving one's neighbor as one's self by feeding the hungry, visiting the sick, clothing the naked, and eliminating the causes of social injustice. These actions are to be taken not as means for evangelism but as ends in themselves. The national body of The Church of the Brethren is a prime example of this. The Church has a strong emphasis on peace, which includes resistance to military service and a completely nonviolent approach to all aspects of life. The Church also has eight affiliated colleges which offer "Peace Studies" as a college major or minor. The Church sponsors day care centers, public forums, disaster relief crews, and lunch programs for the elderly. Conversely, the Church of the Brethren has no written creed or established dogma regarding salvation, baptism, the deity of Christ, or prayer.

General practitioner churches give equal attention to evangelism, teaching, relationships and social action. In contrast to a singleness of purpose they emphasize the need for balance and for non-specializing the Christian life. They attempt to carry out each of Christ's major mandates and at the same time appeal to a broader range of needs and persons. Most churches view this model as the ideal. In fact, many who from an outsider's perspective have extreme emphases, insist that the "balance" in their congregation appeals to all types.

Special purpose churches structure programming around a single issue or style of ministry. Because they have either an extreme theological emphasis or a unique, charismatic leader, congregations of this type cause the average churchgoer to feel uncomfortable. Some examples are churches that attract disproportionate numbers of single adults, university students, handicapped persons, widows, or migrant workers or congregations that emphasize the training of lay persons for ministry and service.

Forum churches are proud of their philosophical diversity. In contrast to specialty churches, they offer a rich variety of subjects and beliefs. Unlike the general practitioner church, however, they do not have a consensus concerning purpose, philosophy or theology. In fact they believe that sophisticated audiences demand tolerance. Since every subject can be viewed in more than one manner, none is allowed preeminence. In large forum churches, staff are assigned more for their distinctive views than for their compatibility with other program ministers. It is not surprising, therefore, that congregations with this mentality are frequently polarized into conservative and liberal wings. Of all the styles listed here forum churches have the greatest growth obstacles to overcome. Although to a less degree, *social action* churches must also face unfavorable odds.

Two other contrasting types are worth noting at the close of this section on philosophical style. First, there is the *propositional church,* that sees people, situations, and issues in absolute categories. A person is acceptable or unacceptable, right or wrong, in the church or outside the church. Although the Bible is used to support each proposition, more emphasis is placed on explaining and applying the message in concrete terms than on letting the book speak for itself.

Conversely, *dynamically equivalent churches* describe truth in terms of non-fixed images. Experiencing is a higher value than explaining, progress is more important than precision, and motives are more essential than meanings.

B. A second means of classifying churches' beliefs is according to *ecclesiastical-historical families.* Because no universal categories exist, a composite grouping, based upon several authorities on American religion, is shown below. It contains nine basic types:

Fundamentalist churches are characterized by rigid interpretations of Scripture and life and by their tendency to denounce other biblical interpretation and lifestyles as heretical.

Evangelical churches stress the authority of Scriptures rather than the authority of the church, allowing for elasticity of personal beliefs and behavior beyond a certain set of essential creeds.

Holiness churches are linked historically to Wesley's doctrine of sanctification, with its focus on the attainment of Christian purity, perfect love, and a life of disciplined devotion to God. The major denominations that have not become Pentecostal in focus are the Missionary Alliance, the Free Methodist, and the Church of the Nazarenes.

Pentecostal churches have evolved from the holiness movement and insist that sanctification is manifested by speaking in tongues. The main Pentecostal denominations are the Assemblies of God, the Churches of God, the Pentecostal Holiness Church and the international Church of the Foursquare Gospel. Some analysts describe the relative rigidity of Pentecostal doctrine and worship as symptomatic of third generation reactional theology.

Charismatic churches are the most recent group to emerge in American churches. They can be distinguished from Pentecostal churches by their greater tolerance of denominational structures and of individuals who may or may not speak in tongues. They are less demonstrative than Pentacostals and focus on first generation spiritual renewal. Charismatic churches can be found within every major denomination. At the present, there are no denominations that are comprehensively charismatic.

Mainline churches belong to the major denominations, with the exception of the Baptists. For the most part they grew rapidly during the last half of the 19th century and became increasingly pluralistic during the middle of the 20th century. This category includes Episcopalians, Congregationalists, Presbyterians, Lutherans, and Methodists, all of which have been declining in membership since 1970.

Baptist churches must be considered as a major category in themselves, due to their distinct autonomy as well as their present number of congregations. They have more than twice as many members as any other denominational family. There are 16 distinct Baptist denominations of significant size and at least 12 others which are considerably smaller. Most of them are either fundamentalist or evangelical in their theology; a few are charismatic; some are essentially mainline in regard to their overall philosophy of ministry.

Catholic churches include all orthodox churches that have preserved an apostolic succession of bishops. The main two groups in the United States are the Roman Catholics and the Eastern Orthodox. A certain percentage of local parishes in each case can be considered evangelical in their theology and some of them are clearly charismatic.[1]

Cultic churches are those which place an extra Scriptural source of authority in an equal or greater position to the Bible, which devaluate Christ's deity and mission, and which perceive themselves as *the* exclusive community of the saved. The largest three in the United States are the Jehovah Witnesses, Church of Jesus Christ of Latter Day Saints, and the Church of Christ, Scientist.

COMPOSITION

Three categories have been identified for classifying churches according to the type of people they contain. They are grouped here by *heritage,* by *creativity* and by *progressiveness.* Other areas of membership composition that could be typified include gradations of age, sex, education, income, vocation, expressed values, and lifestyle manifestations.

A. *The heritage category* refers to the ethnic-geographic background of members. Evolutionary patterns can be observed for the following four definite types.

Indigenous churches use forms of Christian expression that correspond with local culture. Their message is essentially biblical, but their liturgy and lifestyle patterns are uniquely tied to the value system of a single culture. Growth potential is limited to the size of the particular cultural community, which is often only a small portion of a major urban or rural area. In one sense they are a Christianized form of the nativistic movement, often with ambiguous orthodoxy. Two Southern California examples are Chuck Smith's Calvary Chapel of Costa Mesa and Robert Schuller's Crystal Cathedral. In Schuller's books and sermons and televised broadcasts the emphasis of message is upon "emotional and mental strength" rather than biblical lessons.

Ethnic churches are transplanted indigenous congregations whose membership is drawn from one distinct ethnic background. In the majority of cases their roots are in Africa, Europe, Asia, or Latin America. However, they also include migrations from Oklahoma, Arkansas, New York and West Virginia. Some use a native language exclusively, others contain a majority of bilingual members, and some are predominantly English-speaking. A church ceases to be an ethnic church when it has more than 50 percent of its members from other cultural backgrounds.[2]

Heritage churches trace their origin to one distinct ethnic group, but have since absorbed more than 50 percent of their members from other cultural backgrounds. Many of their last names can be linked with specific European or Latin American countries, especially for those in leadership positions. Growth potential is strictly limited for the most part to the number of unchurched from the same ethnic group who are presently living within driving distance. A church ceases to be a heritage church when it can no longer be identified by newcomers with its original ethnic group. *Redemption* and *life* are also problems for both heritage and country churches. People leave these congregations because they no longer relate to their newly acquired values. In a real sense, they "graduate" from one type of church and need to find another that conforms more closely to their modified lifestyles and Christian frame of reference.

Conglomerate churches are non-heritage congregations that have come full cycle. They do not contain any recognizable ethnic or indigenous markings. Their "type" can be found in every region of the United States; their identity is essentially non-geographical and non-cultural. In short, they are a true *melange*. Most members join one-by-one as adults, rather than in groups or as children of existing members. Though they contain a determinate proportion of sociological groupings according to age, vocation, income, and educational level, these mixtures could just as easily be found elsehwere.

B. *The creativity category* describes the tendencies of church leaders toward creating, adapting, and borrowing. Most churches can be placed along a continuum showing three distinct stages.

Programmatic churches accept denominational and para-church programs without alteration. They concentrate on refining the mechanics of implementing programs rather than on making adjustments in order to improve them. Sunday schools use standardized curricula. Congregational profiles generally reveal a low proportion of members who are college graduates, and a high percentage of semi-skilled workers.

Innovative churches have looked at most of the available programs and have modified certain ones to meet their unique situation. Membership consists of predominantly middle-class people with moderate to conservative political convictions.

Conceptual churches have a high percentage of creative leaders who resist adamantly the endorsement of outside programs. Most of their members are professionals and scholars and researchers who work routinely in the field of ideas.

C. *The progressive category* indicates the degree to which members are willing to change their views. Varying proportions of three distinct types can be found in most congregations: *Conservatives* resist all changes initially; they can eventually warm up to new ideas, but with great caution; *Progressives* are advocates of change which occurs gradually, often with the help of a systematic plan; *Radicals* are extremists who insist upon widespread reforms at the earliest opportunity.

These previous six types were first presented by consultant John Wimber, of the Fuller Evangelistic Association in Pasadena. Each should be viewed as more or less constant in a given situation. The issue at stake is not so much preferences as appropriateness. For example, it is just as unrealistic to expect programmatic churches to design their own outreach as it is to expect conceptual churches to be pleased with a pre-packaged parachurch program. Strategy approaches need to be selected with such compositional factors in mind.

LEADERSHIP

It is useful to describe the leadership circle in churches according to educational level, amount of experience, family characteristics, talents, compatibility, and operational style. Of the numerous attempts to define leadership patterns, none have been of more practical value than the 14 operational patterns developed by John Grier.[3] Also instructive is Schaller's emphasis upon the influence of birth order, the non-negotiable roles of the senior minister, and an important distinction between "ranchers" and "shepherds." (See Index references to Schaller.)

STRUCTURE

This final internal category deals with the organizational aspects of congregational life. Churches can be categorized structurally according to polity, size, staff, workers, program, people flow, facilities, planning, and finances. The following four types are arranged here as a means of illustration and explanation:

A. *Ecclesiastical polity structures* are commonly defined as *Episcopalian, Presbyterian* and *Congregational.* As rough equivalents to *monarchical, republican,* and *democratic* governmental structures, these three types encompass the major forms of church government since the first century. Congregational polity can in turn be found in two common forms: the *brownistic type,* a pure form where basic decisions are reached by a congregational vote; and the *borrowistic type,* that operated at the local level more along Presbyterian lines—but with deacons instead of elders. Baptist polity has more variation than any other denominational family. It includes both types of congregational structures, as well as an Episcopalian form, where the senior pastor serves as a bishop and committees function more for implementation than for discussion and decisions. Each form has its own set of advantages. However, as a general rule, the larger a congregation becomes, the more it needs to move from a congregational style to a hierarchical style of polity.

B. *Size.* Until recently very little research has been conducted on issues relating to the size of congregations and church growth. With the appearance of *The Multiple Staff and the Larger Church* (Schaller, 1980), much more is now known. The graph of churches found in this chapter shows the seven most common categories, along with the percentage of churches in each.

Fellowships average below 40 for Sunday morning worship. As overgrown small groups, they provide an ideal setting for the kind of spontaneous caring that characterized congregations in the New Testament. Approximately 25 percent of all churches fall into this category. Leadership is controlled invariably by a nucleus of lay persons, rather than a professional minister.

Small churches average between 50 and 100 at worship. Though still managed largely by the laity, they are usually able to hire either a part-time or full-time minister. Inactive members are proportionately few in this size. Approximately 25 percent of all Protestant congregations fall into this category.

Middle-sized churches average between 100 and 175 at worship. With a full-time pastor and part-time secretary, this category is often considered the *optimum size.* Cost effectiveness is highest, real estate and programs are manageable and members are able to relate to one another genuinely and spontaneously. In the middle-sized congregation, represented by about 25 percent of U.S. churches, the pastor performs best as a shepherd sort of leader.

Awkward size churches derive their name from the difficulties they present for pastors. Ten percent of American churches find themselves at this stage, with worship averaging 175 to 225. The membership circle is usually too large to be served by one minister, yet the size of the budget cannot justify a second full-time person. Members often resist perceiving themselves as multiple congregations, and cling to their image of being a single comfortable family. Two worship services are as difficult to accept as two ministers. Inactive members are not uncommon.

Large churches average between 225 and 450 at worship and account for about 10 percent of the total number of congregations. Multiple staff and multiple services are the rule rather than the exception. Conflicts are more prevalent in this category, and often revolve around questions of purpose, allocation of finances, and roles of individual staff members. Growth difficulties also occur because of the changes that are required in the decision making process, in the role of senior minister and in the development of a more diverse program.

Huge churches represent only four percent of all congregations in America, and average 450 to 700 at wor-

Figure 13

CLASSIFYING PROTESTANT CHURCHES BY SIZE

25%

Fellowship
15-50

25%

Small
50-100

25%

Middle-sized
100-175

10%

Awkward Size
175-225

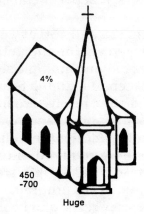

10%

225
-450

Large

4%

450
-700

Huge

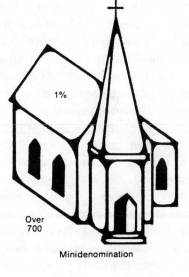

1%

Over
700

Minidenomination

Source: Shaller 1980:27-35

ship. They are viewed as pacesetters in the community and among their denominational executives. With a history of multiple staffing, they are usually well organized and able to offer special programs in music, outreach, education and youth. On the other hand, their cumbersome size requires a greater staffing ratio per 100 members and a larger amount of energy to move forward. Unique difficulties include recruitment of volunteers, squabbles over space, lack of spontaneous gatherings, preoccupation with real estate and maintenance matters, inappropriate matching of pastors and people, and vulnerability in response to crises, especially changes in the senior minister.

Minidenominations, sometimes referred to as *mega* or *super churches,* are congregations that average more than 700 at worship. Only one percent of America's churches deal with the awesome figures of this "big business" category. In addition to the difficulties described for huge congregations, these conglomerate structures must face the criticisms of theologians, fellow pastors, and the press.[4] There is also more a tendency here to build programming around the magnetic personality of the senior minister, such as has been done in the 1980s around men like Jerry Falwell, Robert Schuller, Rex Humbard, and Oral Roberts.

C. *Architecture types.* A third classification of structural distinctions relate to the type of meeting place. In this category Howard Snyder is credited with the identification of four different types: *body churches*—those that hold no property; *cathedral churches*—those that perceive buildings as the focal point; *tabernacle churches*—those that view buildings as primarily functional; and *phantom churches*—those that structure impromptu gatherings and refuse to identify with *any* building.

D. *People flow.* The subjects of assimilation and incorporation were discussed at length in the previous chapter. Two types of churches were introduced which make up this fourth structural category. *Side door churches* concentrate on meeting non-Christians outside the church. Conversions and initial nurture also occur in the community until enough acculturation has occurred so that both the convert and the congregation feel comfortable together. Conversely, *front door churches* draw new members through the worship service by making their program attractive to outsiders. Conversion and nurture both occur after the non-Christian has visited the church (Reeves 1977:14-15, 22).

Several other differences are worth noting. Changes occur more slowly in front door churches than side door churches; longevity is less important in side door congregations. The *popular* approaches of front door churches have the inbuilt danger of becoming ends rather than means.

CHURCH HEALTH

We noted in an earlier reference the various "diseases" a church could suffer from (see index references to Wagner). The health of a church is of prime concern to the church growth analyst, for it best provides a picture of the church's overall potential.

II. UNOFFICIAL CHURCH TYPOLOGIES

With the advancement of media communications and the sociological restructuring of age groups, a variety of para-church organizations have become extremely popular during the 1980s. Some pastors and congregations laud the works of these groups and praise them as supplements to the home church's work. Other people criticize these groups for becoming church substitutes which salve people's consciousnesses for not becoming active church members. Whether good or bad, these religiously-oriented groups are highly visible and, as such, warrant our examination.

MEDIA CHURCHES

Media churches (also referred to as *electronic churches*) have largely come into existence since the 1970s and as a result of an increase in the quality and quantity of Christian programming for national and local audiences. A recent Gallup survey revealed that as many as 13 percent (5,300,000) of American evangelicals do not attend a recognized local church. It is reasonable to conclude that a high percentage of these "churchless Christians" are actively supporting one of the "national" ministries on television through turning on the switch each week and by responding financially to the various "need incentive" requests. These figures can be confirmed both by the increase in the size of the listening audiences as well as the growing financial base of monthly contributors. Media churches make much of the fact that they offer preaching and song worship without the requirement of membership. Their lack of internal structure and hierarchy appeals to people who desire a spectator membership.

PARA-CHURCH FELLOWSHIPS

Para-church fellowships are acceptable "functional substitutes" for churches and are probably ministering to several million Americans who are not a part of an established local church. With the exception of communion and baptism, these organizations provide for the basic Christian needs of their adherents, including worship, fellowship and instruction. Among such groups are Campus Crusade's student ministries, Young Life, Inter-Varsity Fellowship, and the Navigators.

PRIVATIZED DISCIPLES

Privatized disciples are those who are "born again" Christians, but for a variety of reasons have not been incorporated in a local church, a media church, or a parachurch fellowship. Some prefer to guide their own spiritual pilgrimages and admit a low need for other people. Others have not yet found a group of Christians with which they can comfortably unite.

All three of these unofficial churches constitute a growing concern for church leaders and for those within the church growth movement. Although *churchless Christians* can sometimes demonstrate greater consistency and commitment than those within ecclesiastical bodies, it is nevertheless an incomplete commitment. Biblical Christianity requires a visible association with an established church.

At the same time *privatized religion* represents an enormous potential. Gallup's figures show that 13 percent of evangelicals do not belong to any church; approximately 40 percent do not attend services regularly. Among teenagers who consider themselves "highly religious" only one third attend church. An even greater number of persons of all ages—almost 90 percent—believe that one can be a good Christian and still not attend church. Every indication points to an increase in these trends during the 1980s.

Churches are in a good position to provide solutions. They can help by striving to overcome the status quo; by seeking genuine renewal; by countering the misconceptions with a demonstration of concern; and by designing new programming with the needs of churchless Christians in mind. Some, of course, are legitimate media Christians. A certain percentage are unable to attend church for physical or emotional reasons. Included in this category are one million victims of agoraphobia—individuals psychologically unable to mingle with crowds.

Because of the enormous variety of actual situations, it is doubtful that a single taxonomy will ever be adequate. Similarly, the weighting of types for importance will likely remain an open question. Missiologists of varying degrees of competency, perceive even the same phenomena with different interpretations of reality. In spite of these variations, it is hoped that a central body of church types will surface with widespread applications.

Footnotes for Chapter 7

1. Ralph Martin describes this grouping as the *model of the theater* (1980:114-118). Gallup shows how that as a form of worship the Mass is holding steady (1978:5). As in other categories lines cannot be clearly drawn. For some insightful sub-classifying, see Quebedeaux's description of evangelicals who are charismatic, fundamental, and *neo-evangelical* (1978:6-9). Other researchers now use the terms orthodox, conversionalists, and orthodox/conversionalists to iden-tify specific varieties of evangelicals (Gallup 1980:28). For some minor differences between Baptist and fundamental churches see Towns (1973) and Skelton (1974).

2. *Black churches* are the largest ethnic church in America. See Frazier (1973), Mitchell (1975), and Hefley (1977:68-88). For other ethnic descriptions, see Hudson (1970), Te Selle (1973), Greeley (1974 and 1975), Belew (1974), Ellison (1974), and Eames (1977).

3. A considerable range of Grier's self-interpreting tools is available from Performac Systems International, Inc., 5851 Duluth Street, Minneapolis, MN 55422.

4. One of the more insightful critiques is offered by Ralph Martin, who refers to this type as the *corporation model* (1980:118-19). In addition, the "we're big enough" syndrome often emerges as an ef-fective counterforce to the forward momentum of such well lubricated machines (Schuller 1974:34). Organizational structures in mega churches are invariably hierarchical. Schuller calls this type the *Cyprian* perspective, and contrasts it to the less appropriate models of the Anabaptists and of Robert C. Worley. See also his description of the difference between large and small churches, and his analysis of five multiple staff models: *master craftsman-apprentice, relational, paternalistic, functional, clergy vs. lay,* and *clergy couples* (1980:15-50, 85-96). For another set of size classifications see Orjala (1978:91-94).

CHAPTER EIGHT
Future Issues Affecting Church Growth

Since church growth cannot occur instantly, but is, instead, realized over a period of time, church leaders who are interested in seeing growth must be future oriented. They must be willing to think about the social, financial, political, and educational changes that are expected to transpire in the coming months and years. As one business executive recently noted in a popular periodical, "When it comes to the future, an attitude of *que sera, sera* will only lead to failure."

The great essayist George Santayana once wrote, "Those who ignore history are doomed to repeat it." More recently, authors such as Alvin Toffler *(Future Shock, The Third Wave)* and Aurelio Peccei *(One Hundred Pages for the Future)* have counterpointed Santayana by insisting that those who do not make projections about the future are doomed to find themselves in it before they are ready for it.

In a very real sense, all Christians are futurists. Born-again believers all look for the coming return of Christ and many enjoy studying such books of the Bible as Daniel and Revelation to find what God has to reveal about the coming ages.

But the Bible also insists that Christians should be pragmatic. Early Christians were admonished not to sit and simply wait for the return of Christ but instead to be busy witnessing and evangelizing. This, obviously, called for training, planning and working. Modern Christians are not released from these same obligations and responsibilities. This is especially true of those Christian leaders who have a mission to plan for and bring about church growth.

FIND A NEED

In assessing the roles and missions of the church in the coming years, it is wise to recall the first law of business: ''Find a need and fill it.''

While it is a given fact that all the world *needs* to accept the saving grace of Jesus Christ, that fact alone will not always compel new people to attend a church. Frequently it is the meeting of another need—friendship, counseling, activities, fellowship—which first draws the newcomer to a congregation. For this reason, today's churches must attempt to project what tomorrow's community needs will be.

One only needs to pick up a newspaper or magazine or to turn on the radio or television to realize that people in the latter quarter of the twentieth century have rising spiritual expectations (Gallup 1978a:1). Furthermore, people are beginning to expect churches to discuss issues such as abortion, nuclear armament, separation of church and state, genetic human engineering, and literary censorship. The people are wondering how prepared America's ecclesiastical institutions are to provide answers for the questions and problems the population will soon have to deal with. The response the church makes will have a definite impact on its growth potential.

This book has attempted to shed light on the matter of where the churches have come from, where and why they are flourishing, and where they appear to be moving in the immediate future. The present direction is far from uniform. Many churches prefer to remain in the first half of the 20th century rather than attempt to move forward. Overall, more churches are plateauing or declining rather than growing. For those that are growing, the potential pitfalls are numerous. And for those who seek to aid the church, the issues are highly complex.

Several warnings are needed, therefore, as the church growth effort proceeds in coming generations. First, future approaches must remain *solidly rooted in biblical theology.* Strategies must not be designed by those with a low view of Scripture or a diluted sense of mission. Second, church growth principles should maintain an *interdisciplinary perspective.* As a relatively new movement in America, its cutting edge must not be blunted by a crystallization of present concepts. Continuous interaction will further enhance the effectiveness of its methods. Correctives from future new disciplines will be needed. In order to help churches avoid using philosophical rationalization in place of contextual and institutional factors, new studies and stances will be required.

Third, caution should be taken to see that innovative approaches continue to be *built upon diachronic constructs.* Ethno-historical considerations will be increasingly prominent as minority group lobbying raises the level of ethnic consciousness among the Christian public. A time perspective will further help to minimize the promotion of peripheral issues that are fascinating, but unfruitful.[1] Similarly, additional research into comparative ecclesiology must be done to provide improved options for intentional programming. Diachronic models can serve as useful yardsticks (Tippet 1973a:441-46). 1973a:441-46).

Fourth, future church growth development should be the *result of the pragmatic integration of ideas.* Armchair theology will be less effective in this respect than contact theology. In-house specialists will be more useful than general theoreticians. Those who can synthesize and reconceptualize will be in greater demand than those who merely speculate in isolation. Above all, data retrieval will have to be developed in a manner which will make needed information readily accessible to contribute to effective problem solving in local churches. Prescriptive approaches will gradually replace patent approaches. Future publications and seminars will be geared increasingly to adaptation more than dissemination.

The above predictions will serve as a backdrop as we now address some major concerns of the near future.

PRESERVING PRINCIPLES

The issue raised here is many sided, but it especially relates to handling changes in the larger society without hurting smaller "church societies." For example, almost every congregation is affected to some degree by the currently changing roles of women, husbands, and families. The implications of such movements on ministry opportunities are staggering. Churches unwilling to adapt are sometimes oblivious to the point of paralysis. At the same time, tolerant and "liberated" congregations must learn to respect the strictness factors required in the maintenance of meaning. Not all congregations will strike the same balance between the need to tighten up and share common values and the propensity for relaxing standards and permitting autonomy and diversity.

Frequently overlooked is the need to develop *change agent sensitivities.* The reason one church experiences resistance while another experiences renaissance can be due to different perceptions of the change process. As a general rule, a new concept should be presented only when a congregation is completely sympathetic to the person who is speaking—the higher the degree of suspicion, the greater the need to exercise caution. Effecting change requires church leaders adept at explaining things well and congregations willing to listen (Tippett

1973b:122-123). At the national level the efforts of church growth directors are often ineffective because they present a real or imagined threat to established procedures. In both cases communication could be improved by applying principles of change.[2]

ADDITIONAL ECCLESIOLOGISTS

Only recently have churches started to realize that specialists are required to deal with matters of congregational health, potential, and planning. Consequently, the need for church practitioners, or *ecclesiologists,* can be anticipated to increase substantially in future decades (Wagner 1979d:286-287). Although pastors may become more proficient in self-diagnosis and problem solving, they will no longer be able to single-handedly shoulder the responsibilities for managing the growth process.

An ecclesiologist, in a strict sense, is neither a consultant nor a mission strategist. Traditionally, the former group of professionals have dealt with churches primarily from their organizational development stages. Mission strategists, on the other hand, have devoted themselves for the most part to cross cultural matters in foreign lands. Ecclesiologists combine the cross cultural expertise of mission development with the special aptitude and training of church consultants.

In the next decade a growing number of graduate institutions will be expected to have faculty members with doctoral degrees in church growth.[3] Such policy shifts will enable those responsible for the preparation of ministers to deal with this subject as a whole, rather than from a strictly theological or pastoral perspective. The scope of topics will undoubtedly be broadened to include case studies, field trips to growing churches, and ongoing ministry assignments with both personal and peer accountability.

In designing these courses the curriculum planners will have to be innovative and progressive. They will need to offer more than just a rehash of various mission theories that no longer will be applicable. Courses in trend analyses, demographics, public relations, media production, advertising, direct mail operations, telephone canvassing, and survey taking will all need to be developed in order to train future church growth specialists how to cope with coming social and technological developments.

Through insistence upon such unswerving criteria, institutions will be able to discern the difference between aspiring ecclesiologists—those who will gather hard data and write dissertations—and actual ecclesiologists—those who will demonstrate a consistent ability to help churches draw and incorporate a larger percentage of unchurched residents. Such a course should be so disciplined that certification for a graduate will not be granted until a reasonable period of internship has been completed.[4]

GLOBAL OUTREACH

A growing number of mission strategists now believe that it is both biblically expedient and technically feasible to give every person in the world the opportunity to become a Christian; yet, there are almost insurmountable limits to such globalistic abstractions. As has been shown, the world consists not of a single monolithic and technological society but rather of thousands of particularistic peoples (Reeves 1977b:155-156). In the United States the mandate will at last be completed only through planning broad in scope yet local in specific design.

In order to be effective these plans will need to recognize the reality of differing value systems. They will have to consider the numerous obstacles, institutional-ly and contextually, that are capable of thwarting achievement.

On the other hand, church planning should seek, where possible, to relate positively to the recurring human needs of this hour: family problems, economic and financial difficulties, unemployment, illness, education of children, retirement plans, energy shortages, relocation due to job changes, and loneliness (Gallup 1978a:6).

Furthermore, planning can anticipate the kinds of demographic shifts that are presently occurring among two types of city folk. One group is arriving in densely populated centers from other geographical locations, while a second group is leaving the cities to resettle in rural areas. Congregations that specifically reach out to new arrivals will continue to reap a spiritual harvest throughout the last quarter of this century.

There are three more ideas which can be used to assist church growth efforts in the future. First, an emphasis on ministry to particular segments of the population could help to eliminate strife within American Christendom. Because of the pluralistic nature of religion in the United States, biblical Christianity ought not to exert too much energy in seeking to convert various strands to alternative formulations of Christianity. Such shiftings will occur automatically as discontented church members search for institutions that correspond more to their personal preferences. A much greater need is to project the Christian message outward, rather than inward, toward receptive unchurched pockets of Americans.

A second idea is for the particularity of mainline denominations to be viewed as a strength rather than a weakness. In planning for a reversal of present downward trends, mainline churches should not seek to compete directly with the newer, more conservative denominations. Instead, they should start innovative ministries among the unchurched who are within their unique spheres of influence.

Finally, there is the idea that all groups seeking to fulfill the Great Commission should concentrate on creating highly particular strategies. In most cases this will necessitate the development of new resources. As a series of initial steps, church leaders should be encouraged to explore the multitude of possibilities: the establishment of an accessible church growth library; participation in regional or local church growth seminars; and the gathering of data for trend assessments, either through a variety of self helps[5] or by outside specialists. Once new possibilities are identified and selected, leaders then can begin the process of creating and redesigning programs. Ideally, matters relating to the ultimate role of a congregation's ministry should then be addressed, and culminated in the formulation of a realistic master plan.

Truly, church growth is future oriented. It needs to be planned in relation to the future because it is the hope of the future.

Footnotes for Chapter 8

1. Definitive church growth perspectives on emerging fields such as *planetology* (McFadden 1976:230-244) and *feminine theology* (McNamara 1974:402-408) would be premature. However, a diachronic framework helps to minimize anxiety in these matters until they become widespread issues.

2. In addition to Barnett (1953) and Schaller (1972), see Lippett (1958), Goodenough (1963), Fabun (1970), Zimbardo and Ebbeson (1970), and Sarason (1972).

3. This trend will be a further indication that, as a science, church growth has entered a second generation. Academic disciplines do not as a rule reach maturity until faculty members hold doctorates from the same specialized field.

4. Such convictions are based upon the observation that traditional ministerial courses do not ensure effectiveness in pastoral performance. Corrective steps are needed in the entire process: selection of the right students, the right faculty, and the right curriculum; and the establishment of an ongoing process of monitoring, evaluating, and supplemental training. For other radical suggestions, see McGavran and Arn (1977:103-104).

5. Local church seminars are advertised frequently in Christian periodicals. The Institute for American Church Growth (150 South Los Robles, Pasadena, California 91101) and the Charles E. Fuller Institute (44 South Mentor, Pasadena, California 91102) both offer church growth training for professionals and lay leaders.

BEST BOOKS ON FUTURE ISSUES

Because history contains some of the best counsel concerning future issues, several classic works have been included in this selection of recommended reading.

1. AHLSTROM, Sydney D.
   1975 *A Religious History of the American People,* Doubleday Garden City, New York. (M)
2. DAYTON, Edward R. and David A. Frazier
   1980 *Planning Strategies for World Evangelization,* Eerdmans, Grand Rapids. (M)
3. DUBOSE, Francis M., ed.
   1980 *Classics of Christian Missions,* Broadman, Nashville. (H)
4. HANDY, Robert T.
   1977 *A History of the Churches in the United States and Canada,* Oxford University Press, New York. (M)
5. KRAUS, C. Norman
   1980 *Missions, Evangelism and Church Growth,* Herald Press, Scottdale, Penn. (M)
6. McFADDEN, Thomas M., ed.
   1976 *America In Theological Perspective,* Seabury Press, New York. (H)
7. McNAMARA, Patrick M., ed.
   1974 *Religion American Style,* Harper and Row, New York. (H)
8. MARTY, Martin T.
   1976 *A Nation of Behavers,* University of Chicago Press, Chicago. (M)
9. PIEPKORN, Arthur C.
   1978 *Profiles in Belief: The Religious Bodies of the United States and Canada,* Vols. 1-4, Harper and Row, New York.
10. SCHULLER, David S., Merton P. Strommen, and Milo L. Brekke, eds.
    1980 *Ministry in America,* Harper and Row, San Francisco. (H)
11. WAGNER, C. Peter
    1981 *Church Growth and the Whole Gospel,* Harper and Row, New York.
12. WOODBRIDGE, John D.
    1975 *The Evangelicals: What They Believe, Who They Are, Where They Are Changing,* Abingdon, Nashville. (M)

APPENDIX A
Synthesis of Classic Church Growth Debates

A. *The Objections*

1. *Non-evangelical criticisms*—from those who are liberal theologically, or who subscribe to universalism.

    a.   Presence is more important than proselytism.

    b.   Brotherhood must take priority over the new birth.

    c.   Dialogue is more urgently needed than discipling.

    d.   The irrelevancy of churches is more certain than the imperativeness of churches.

    e.   Foreign missions must be content with establishing bridgeheads rather than perpetuating church multiplication.

    f.   The New Testament does not give a clear mandate for mission.[1]

2. *Non-spiritual criticisms*—from those who believe that church growth theology is too secular.

    a.   Church growth is based more on humanistic theories than on spiritual values.

    b.   All church problems are essentially spiritual in nature and require spiritual solutions.

    c.   The field of missions is God's responsibility, and man must be careful to not interfere.

    d. Numbers are not important—quality is a higher value than quantity.

    e. Church growth is too scientific and too impersonal.

    f. Church growth is heavily seasoned with American pragmatism and capitalistic technology.

    g. The end does not always justify the means—it is better to not Christianize at all than to Christianize on dubious grounds.

    h. Missions cannot be selective—everyone must have equal priority to hear the Gospel.

3. *Non-biblical criticisms*—from those who believe that the church growth movement is not sufficiently biblical.

    a. Church growth lacks theological depth —its hermeneutics are particularly shallow.

    b. Theology is more message than ministry.

    c. The theological focus should be Christ rather than the Church.

    d. Mission cannot be truncated into discipling and perfecting—this emphasis is both unnecessary and confusing.

    e. Task-oriented triumphalism must be tempered by relational sensitivities.

    f. Church growth theology encourages nominality by condoning various kinds of "cheap grace"—counting the cost of Christian commitment is rarely emphasized.

    g. More emphasis should be placed on Christian education.

4. *Non-practical criticisms*—from those who question the tangible contributions of the movement to churches and missions.

a. Church growth is strong in diagnosis but weak in prognosis—it remains to be seen how much practical differences its efforts can produce.

b. The movement contains an overly innovative linguistic style—it often disregards the rules of linguistic derivation—its unnecessary redefining of terms results in a tactical gumming-up of conversations.

5. *Mono-cultural criticisms*—from those who de-emphasize cultural diversity.

a. Church growth theology contains a clever disguise for racism.

b. The movement places too much emphasis on culture in general.

c. Cultural tolerance often leads to syncretism.

d. There is an anthropological-functionalistic syndrome inherent in the movement—it must be balanced by greater input from the field of social psychology.[2]

e. People movements produce shallow converts—discipleship involves concentrated one-on-one instructions.

B. *The Rebuttals*

Church growth scholars have not been insensitive to these criticisms. Indeed, in some instances their responses could be described in retrospect as over-reactionary. However, whether by standing before a theological firing squad or by serenely browsing subterranean libraries, a significant amount of refutations have been accumulated by those who subscribe to the mission theology of Donald McGavran. A representative sample is listed below in corresponding categories.

1. *To the non-evangelical*

    a. "Church Growth and Theology," by Arthur F. Glasser in *God, Man and Church Growth,* Alan Tippett, ed., pp. 52-67.

    b. "Theological Issues," in Donald McGavran's *Crucial Issues in Mission's Tomorrow* (ed.), Part I, pp. 33-121.

    c. *Verdict Theology in Missionary Theory,* Alan R. Tippett, pp. 37-116.

    d. *Shaken Foundations,* pp. 34-62 and *Missions, Which Way,* pp. 1-42, both by Peter Beyerhaus.

    e. "Dialogue," John R. W. Stott, in *Christian Mission in the Modern World,* pp. 58-73.[3]

2. *To the spiritually oriented*

    a. "Basic Considerations," Part I of Donald McGavran's *Understanding Church Growth,* pp. 13-65.

    b. "Problems of Non-Growth," Chapter 3 of Alan Tippett's *Church Growth and the Word of God,* pp. 47-57.

    c. "Is Numerical Church Growth a Most Crucial Task in Missions," and "Is it Right for the Church to Concentrate on the Responsive Elements of Society," both in J. Robertson McQuilken's *Measuring the Church Growth Movement,* pp. 19-33, 34-43.

    d. "The Role of the Holy Spirit in Church Growth," by John T. Seamonds in *God, Man and Church Growth,* pp. 95-107.

3. *To the biblically concerned*

    a. "Church Growth as a Biblical Concept," Chapter 1 of Alan Tippett's *Church Growth and the Word of God,* pp. 9-25.

b.   "Theological Issues," in Donald McGavran's *Church Growth and Christian Mission* (ed.), Part I, pp. 27-67.

c.   "God Wants Your Church to Grow," and "What is Church Growth All About?," both in C. Peter Wagner's *Your Church Can Grow,* pp. 34-42 and 161-171.

d.   "Perfection Growth," by Alan Gates in *God, Man and Church Growth,* pp. 128-141.

4. *To the pragmatist*

a.   "Will Large Growth Result from Using Church Growth Principles and Techniques?" J. Robertson McQuilken in *Measuring the Church Growth Movement,* pp. 67-72.

b.   "How to Get Out of a Holding Pattern," Charles Chaney and Ron Lewis in *Design for Church Growth,* pp. 65-84, and "How to Turn Your Growth Curve Straight Up," pp. 141-164.

c.   "Targeting for Maximum Growth," and "Preparing for Sustained Growth," Paul Orjala in *Get Ready to Grow,* pp. 61-100.

d.   "Plan a Strategy for Growth," Waldo J. Werning in *Vision and Strategy for Church Growth,* pp. 52-63.

e.   "Greetings From Down Under," Kevin Crawford in *Church Growth: America,* January-February, 1977, pp. 11-16.

5. *To the mono-culturalist*

a.   "The Dynamics of Church Growth," Chapter 2 in Alan Tippett's *Church Growth and the Word of God,* pp. 28-46.

b.   "Sociological Issues," Part II in Donald McGavran's *Church Growth and Christian Mission,* pp. 69-109

c.   "Christianity and Culture: Biblical Bedrock,"
      Lloyd Kwast in *God, Man and Church Growth*,
      pp. 159-163.

d.   "Are People Movement Conversions Valid?"
      and "Are Anthropological Studies Legitimate
      for Evangelism," both in J. Robertson
      McQuilkin's *Measuring the Church Growth
      Movement*, pp. 44-49 and 50-66.

Notes for Appendix A

1. This view insists that the Gospels are devoid of any commission to the Gentiles. It also suggests that the missionary epoch ended with the death of Peter and Paul, since no missionary purpose is stated in the epistles (see Ferdinand Hahn's *Mission in the New Testament* (1965:139-141). Although highly technical, one of the most thorough rebuttals to this position can be found in Joachim Jeremias' *Jesus' Promise to the Nations* (1958:9-74).

2. This criticism is not strictly limited to mono-culturalists. Together with the concern for the weakness of church growth prognosis (4a), this observation, in the opinion of the author, contains the greatest substance.

3. Even though Beyerhaus and Stott cannot be considered as church growth spokesmen, their theological views on this aspect of missions are essentially compatible with most of the leaders within the movement.

APPENDIX B

Popular Lists of Church Growth Principles/Factors

During the formative 1970s a great deal of literature was generated with an aim toward distilling the essence or "secrets" of growing churches. The following lists are taken from sixteen books which are representative of such "principle listing" results. Notice the overlap as well as the distinctives of each institutional factor cited. Chapter 1 of *Always Advancing* has attempted to extract and to synthesize the most strategic variables.

1. Wendell Belew (1971)

   1. A definite purpose
   2. Authoritative leadership
   3. A developed growth strategy
   4. An understanding of their community
   5. People involvement

2. Harold Fickett (1972)

   1. Christ centered
   2. Biblically based
   3. Evangelistic
   4. Regenerated membership
   5. Confidence in leadership
   6. Scripturally financed
   7. Adequately staffed
   8. Motivated by faith
   9. Diversified in service
   10. Balanced in emphases

3. Robert Schuller (1974)

    1. Accessibility
    2. Surplus parking
    3. Inventory
    4. Service
    5. Visibility
    6. Possibility thinking
    7. Good cash flow

4. Lyle Schaller (1975)

    1. Bible preaching
    2. Emphasis on evangelism
    3. Changing membership fellowship circle
    4. Opportunities to commitment
    5. Imported leadership
    6. Specialties in ministry
    7. Minister who likes people

5. Leroy Lawson and Tetsunao Yamamori (1975)

    1. The Christians really believe
    2. The Christians want their church to grow
    3. The Christians expect their church to grow
    4. The Holy Spirit empowers the church to grow
    5. Dynamic Christians lead growing churches
    6. Christians win their own families
    7. Christian members win their own kind
    8. New Christians are carefully taught
    9. New Christians go immediately to work
    10. Churches rise to the challenge of change
    11. The Church belongs to the people
    12. Christians ask God for church growth

6. C. Peter Wagner (1976)

    1. The pastor
    2. The people of the church
    3. Church size

    4.   Structure and function
    5.   Homogeneous units
    6.   Methods
    7.   Priorities

7.   Bernard and Marjorie Palmer (1976)

    1.   Analysis and evaluation
    2.   Strong Bible emphases
    3.   Love
    4.   Dynamic leadership
    5.   Adaptability
    6.   Program

8.   Foster Shannon (1977)

    1.   A desire to grow
    2.   A pastor committed to growth
    3.   Lengthy pastorates
    4.   Regular membership classes
    5.   Programs designed to reach the unchurched

9.   C. B. Hogue (1977)

    1.   Phenomena: the indomitable dream
    2.   Purpose: extend or perish
    3.   Principles: biblical dynamics
    4.   Priorities: impossible is possible
    5.   Pastor: the pacesetter
    6.   People: making spectators participators
    7.   Process: 1-fitting system to strategy
    8.   Process: 2-awaking, equipping, developing
    9.   Perils: watch your step!
   10.   Power: the exciting side of Pentecost
   11.   Product: the dream come true

10.   Charles Chaney and Ron Lewis (1977)

    1.   Growing churches know where they are going
    2.   Growing churches focus on homogeneous units

3.   Growing churches mobilize and train the laity
4.   Growing churches have diversified ministries
5.   Growing churches utilize small group dynamics
6.   Growing churches major on direct evangelism
7.   Growing churches go forward in faith

11.   Donald McGavran and Winfield Arn (1977)

1.   Churches grow as they discover church growth principles
2.   Churches grow as they respect biblical principles
3.   Churches grow as they yield themselves to God's unswerving purpose
4.   Churches grow as priorities are given to effective evangelism
5.   Churches grow as they rightly discern the body
6.   Churches grow as they rightly discern the community
7.   Churches grow as they find new groups and ways to disciple
8.   Churches grow as they structure for growth
9.   Churches grow as they risk for growth

12.   Paul Orjala (1978)

1.   Growing churches know where their converts come from
2.   Growing churches plan for results
3.   Growing churches train people for evangelism
4.   Growing churches incorporate new converts into the church
5.   Growing churches utilize multiple channels of ministry
6.   Growing churches specialize in what works best for them

13. Charles Mylander (1979)

   1. Build your church morale
   2. Follow Christ's marching orders
   3. Discover your role in church growth
   4. Close the back door
   5. Focus on your evangelistic bull's-eye

14. Floyd Bartel (1979)

   1. A growing congregation has a deliberate commitment to people beyond itself
   2. A growing congregation knows clearly why it exists
   3. A growing congregation has a climate within that accepts and affirms new persons
   4. A growing church multiplies the number of meaningful groups in the congregation
   5. A growing congregation has accepted evangelism as a basic responsibility of the local church
   6. A growing church has leadership which enables and encourages growth
   7. A growing church faces and deals with obstacles to growth
   8. A growing congregation intentionally plants new churches
   9. A growing congregation seeks to understand itself and analyzes the situation into which God has placed it
   10. A growing congregation plans expectantly
   11. A growing church uses the many gifts of the Spirit for worship, fellowship, and outreach
   12. A growing church trains its members for the tasks to which they are called

15.   George Hunter III (McGavran and Hunter, 1980)

    1.   Finding the bridges of God
    2.   Motivating local church people
    3.   Training the laity for church growth

16.   Ron Jenson and Jim Stevens (1981)

    1.   Prayer: ask and expect God to do the miraculous
    2.   Worship: experience meaningful corporate celebration
    3.   Purpose: unite around common objectives
    4.   Diagnosis: analyze the local church and the community
    5.   Priorities: emphasize important activities and values
    6.   Planning: project ways to achieve objectives
    7.   Programming: build ministries which move toward objectives
    8.   Climate: radiate love, service, witness, and expectancy
    9.   Leadership: motivate and guide toward objectives
    10. Laity: utilize the strengths of individuals
    11. Absorption: establish a strong sense of belonging
    12. Small Groups: develop deep interpersonal relationships
    13. Discipleship: promote commitment and spiritual multiplication
    14. Training: equip with knowledge, skills, and character
    15. Evangelism: present the gospel effectively

BIBLIOGRAPHY

ADAMS, Arthur M.
    1978 *Effective Leadership for Today's Church,* Westminster, Philadelphia.
ADAMS, James Luther
    1966 *Voluntary Associations,* John Knox, Richmond.
AHLSTROM, Sydney E.
    1972 *A Religious History of the American People,* Yale University Press, New Haven.
ALLEN, Roland
    1962 *Missionary Methods: St. Paul's or Ours?* Eerdmans, Grand Rapids.
ALTMAN, Irwin and Dalmas A. Taylor
    1973 *Social Penetration: The Development of Interpersonal Relationships,* Holt, Rinehart & Winston, Inc., New York.
AMBERSON, Talmadge R., ed.
    1979 *The Birth of Churches: A Biblical Base for Church Planting,* Broadman, Nashville.
ANDERSON, James D.
    1973 *To Come Alive,* Harper & Row, New York.
ANDERSON, James D. and Ezra Earl Jones
    1978 *The Management of Ministry,* Harper & Row, San Francisco.
ANDERSON, Phillip and Phoebe Anderson
    1975 *The House Church,* Abingdon, Nashville.
ARMSTRONG, Ben
    1979 *The Electric Church,* T. Nelson, Nashville.
ARN, Winfield C.
    1977 "A Church Growth Look at Here's Life America," *Church Growth America,* January-February.

ARN, Winfield C., ed.
    1979 *The Pastor's Church Growth Handbook,* Church
         Growth Press, Pasadena.
BACKMAN, Milton Vaughn
    1976 *Christian Churches of America: Origins & Beliefs,*
         Brigham Young University Press, Provo, Utah.
BALSWICK, Jack
    1974 "The Jesus People Movement," *Religion American
         Style,* Patrick H. McNamara, ed., Harper & Row, New
         York.
BARBOUR, Ian G.
    1974 *Myths, Models and Paradigms: A Comparative
         Study in Science and Religion,* Harper & Row, New
         York.
BARCLAY, William
    1975 *Turning to God: A Study of Conversion in the Book
         of Acts and Today,* Baker, Grand Rapids.
BARNETT, Homer G.
    1953 *Innovation: Basis of Cultural Change,* McGraw-Hill,
         New York.
BARRETT, D. B.
    1976 "Unreached Peoples Defined," letter from Donald
         McGavran, November 29.
BARTEL, Floyd G.
    1979 *A New Look at Church Growth,* Faith and Life Press,
         Newton, Kansas.
BASSHAM, Rodger
    1979 *Mission Theology,* William Carey, Pasadena.
BATES, Frederick L. and Clyde C. Harvey
    1975 *The Structure of Social Systems,* Gardner Press, New
         York.
BAUMANN, Dan
    1976 *All Originality Makes a Dull Church,* Vision House,
         Santa Ana, California
BEAVER, R. Pierce, ed.
    1977 *American Missions in Bicentennial Perspective,* Wil-
         liam Carey, Pasadena.
BEDEL, George, Leo Sandon and Charles Welborn
    1975 *Religion in America,* Macmillan, New York.

BELEW, M. Wendell
>1971 *Churches and How They Grow,* Broadman, Nashville.
BELEW, M. Wendell, ed.
>1974 *Missions in the Mosaic,* Southern Baptist Convention, Atlanta.
BENJAMIN, Paul
>1972 *The Growing Congregation,* Lincoln Christian College, Lincoln, Illinois.
BENNETT, David and Edward F. Murphy
>1974 *Church Growth and Church Health: Diagnosis and Prescription,* unpublished doctor of ministry thesis, Fuller Theological Seminary, Pasadena.
BERNE, Eric
>1972 *What Do You Say After You Say Hello?,* Grove Press, New York.
>1973 *The Structure and Dynamics of Organizations and Groups,* Ballantine Books, New York.
BEYERHAUS, Peter
>1972 *Shaken Foundations: Theological Foundations for Mission,* Zondervan, Grand Rapids.
BIERSDORF, John E.
>1975 *Hunger for Experience,* The Seabury Press, New York.
BIERSDORF, John E., ed.
>1976 *Creating an Intentional Ministry,* Abingdon, Nashville
BISAGNO, John R.
>1971 *How to Build an Evangelistic Church,* Broadman, Nashville.
BLAUW, Johannes
>1962 *The Missionary Nature of the Church,* McGraw-Hill, New York.
BRAMMER, Lawrence M.
>1973 *The Helping Relationship—Process and Skills,* Prentice-Hall, Englewood Cliffs, New Jersey.
BRAUER, Jerald C.
>1974 *Protestantism in America,* Westminster, Philadelphia.

BRAUN, Neil
    1971 *Laity Mobilized,* Eerdmans, Grand Rapids.
BRIDGE, Donald and David Phypers
    1974 *Spiritual Gifts and the Church,* Inter-Varsity,
        Downers Grove.
BRIGHT, Bill
    1978 "The Great Commission Definition," *Woldwide
        Challenge,* July.
BRIGHT, John
    1953 *The Kingdom of God,* Abingdon, Nashville.
BUEHLER, Herman G.
    1973 *Nominality Considered,* unpublished doctor of mis-
        siology thesis, Fuller Theological Seminary, Pasa-
        dena.
BUHLMANN, Walbert
    1977 *The Coming of the Third Church,* Orbis, Maryknoll.
BURNS, MacGregor
    1978 *Leadership,* Harper & Row, New York.
BYRE, Donn
    1971 *The Attraction Paradigm,* Academic Press, New
        York
CARROLL, Jackson W., Douglas Johnson and Martin Marty
    1978 *Religion in America: 1950-Present,* Harper & Row,
        New York.
CARROLL, Jackson W., ed.
    1977 *Small Churches are Beautiful,* Harper & Row, San
        Francisco.
CHANDLER, E. Russell
    1971 *The Kennedy Explosion,* David C. Cook. Elgin, Illi-
        nois.
CHANEY, Charles L. and Ron S. Lewis
    1977a *Design for Church Growth,* Broadman, Nashville.
    1977b *Manual for Design for Church Growth,* Broadman,
        Nashville.
CHRISTOFF, Nicholas
    1978 *Saturday Night, Sunday Morning: Singles and the
        Church,* Harper & Row, San Francisco.
CLINTON, Bobby
    1980 "Classifying Types of Churches," an exploratory
        research project for C. Peter Wagner at Fuller Theo-
        logical Seminary, Pasadena.

COLLINS, Lyndhurst
    1976 *The Use of Models in the Social Sciences,* Westview
        Press, London.
CONN, Harvie
    1976 *Theological Perspectives on Church Growth,* Pres-
        byterian & Reformed, Nutley, New Jersey.
COOK, Harold R.
    1975 "Who Really Sent the First Missionaries?" *Evangel-
        ical Missions Quarterly,* October.
COSTAS, Orlando E.
    1974 *The Church and Its Mission: A Shattering Critique
        from the Third World,* Tyndale and Coverdale, Lon-
        don and Wheaton.
CROW, Paul A., Jr. and William Jerry Boney, eds.
    1972 *Church Union at Midpoint,* Association Press, New
        York.
DASHEFSKY, Arnold
    1976 *Ethnic Identity in Society,* Rand McNally, Chicago.
DAVIES, J. G., ed.
    1972 *The Westminster Dictionary of Worship,* Westmin-
        ster, Philadelphia.
DAYTON, Edward R.
    1978 *Planning Strategies for Evangelism: A Workbook,*
        MARC, Monrovia, California.
DAYTON, Edward R. and David A. Fraser
    1980 *Planning Strategies For World Evangelization,* Eerd-
        mans, Grand Rapids.
DEASY, C. M.
    1974 *Design for Human Affairs,* Schenkman Publishing
        Company, Cambridge, Massachusetts.
DENISOFF, R. Serge, Orel Callahan and Mark H. Levine, eds.
    1975 *Theories and Paradigms in Contemporary Sociol-
        ogy,* Peacock Publishers, Inc., Itasca, Illinois.
DeRIDDER, Richard R.
    1971 *Discipling the Nations,* Baker, Grand Rapids.
DesPORTES, Elisa L.
    1973 *Congregations in Change,* The Seabury Press, New
        York.
DIETTERICH, Paul and Russell Wilson
    1976 *A Process of Local Church Vitalization,* Center for
        Parish Development, Naperville, Illinois.

DITTES, James E.
    1967 *The Church in the Way,* Charles Scribners Sons,
        New York.
DOW, Robert
    1977 *Ministry with Single Adults,* Judson Press, Valley
        Forge.
DRIGGERS, B. Carlisle
    1977 *The Church in the Changing Community,* Home
        Mission Board, Southern Baptist Convention, At-
        lanta.
DRIGGERS, B. Carlisle, ed.
    1979 *Models of Metropolitan Ministry,* Broadman, Nash-
        ville.
DUBOSE, Francis M.
    1978 *How Churches Grow in an Urban World,* Broadman,
        Nashville.
DUDLEY, Carl S.
    1978 *Making the Small Church Effective,* Abingdon,
        Nashville.
    1979 *Where Have All Our People Gone?,* Pilgrim Press,
        New York.
DULLES, Avery
    1974 *Models of the Church,* Doubleday, Garden City.
    1977 *The Resilient Church,* Doubleday, Garden City.
EAMES, Edwin and Judith Goode
    1977 *Anthropology of the City,* Prentice-Hall, Englewood
        Cliffs, New Jersey.
EARLE, John R., Dean D. Knudsen and Donald W. Shriver
    1976 *Spindles and Spires,* John Knox, Atlanta.
EISENSTADT, S. N. and M. Curelaru
    1976 *The Form of Sociology—Paradigms and Crises,*
        John Wiley and Sons, New York.
EISTER, Allan W., ed.
    1974 *Changing Perspectives in the Scientific Study of
        Religion,* John Wiley and Sons, New York.
ELLISON, Craig W.
    1974 *The Urban Mission,* Eerdmans, Grand Rapids.
ELLWOOD, Robert S.
    1973a *Religious and Spiritual Groups in Modern America,*
        Prentice-Hall, Englewood Cliffs, New Jersey.

1973b *One Way—The Jesus Movement and Its Meaning*, Prentice-Hall, Englewood Cliffs, New Jersey.

ENGEL, James F. and H. Wilbert Norton
1975 *What's Gone Wrong with the Harvest?*, Zondervan, Grand Rapids.

ENGEL, James F., Hugh G. Wales and Martin R. Warshaw
1975 *Promotional Strategy*, Richard D. Irwin, Inc., Homewood, Illinois.

ENGSTROM, Ted W.
1976 *The Making of a Christian Leader*, Zondervan, Grand Rapids.

FABUN, Don
1970 *The Dynamics of Change*, Prentice-Hall, New York.

FELTON, Virgil
1974 *A Manual for New Church Evangelism*, New Churches of Christ Evangelism, Grand Ledge, Michigan.

FEY, Harold, E., ed.
1970 *A History of the Ecumenical Movement 1948-1968*, Westminster, Philadelphia.

FICKETT, Harold, Jr.
1972 *Hope for Your Church*, Regal Books, Glendale.

FLAKE, Arthur
1922 *Building a Standard Sunday School*, Convention Press, Nashville.

FORD, Julienne
1975 *Paradigms and Fairy Tales: An Introduction to the Science of Meanings*, Routledge and Kegan Paul, London.

FRAZIER, E. Franklin
1973 *The Negro Church in America*, Schoken Press, New York.

FREYTAG, Justus and Kenji Ozaki
1970 *Nominal Christianity*, Letterworth, London.

FULLER EVANGELISTIC ASSOCIATION, Department of Church Growth
1976 *The Biblical Basis for Church Growth*, Fuller Evangelistic Association, Pasadena.

GALLUP, George
1978a *Religion in America*, Princeton Religious Research

Center, Princeton, New Jersey

1978b *The Unchurched American*, Princeton Religious Research Center, Princeton, New Jersey.

1980 "Attitudes Toward Winning the World for Christ," *Christianity Today*, July.

GASTIL, Raymond D.

1975 *Cultural Regions of the United States*, University of Washington Press, Seattle.

GATES, Alan

1973 "Perfection Growth," *God, Man and Church Growth*, Alan R. Tippett, ed., Eerdmans, Grand Rapids.

GAUSTAD, Edwin Scott

1974 *A Religious History of America*, Harper & Row, New York.

1976 *Historical Atlas of Religion in America*, Harper & Row, New York.

GENTRY, Gardiner

1976 *Bus Them In*, Baker, Grand Rapids.

GERBER, Vergil

1973 *God's Way to Keep a Church Going and Growing*, Regal Books, Glendale.

GETZ, Gene A.

1974 *Sharpening the Focus of the Church*, Moody, Chicago.

GLASSE, James D.

1972 *Putting It Together in the Parish*, Abingdon, Nashville.

GLASSER, Arthur

1973 "Church Growth and Theology," *God, Man & Church Growth*, Alan R. Tippett, ed., Eerdmans, Grand Rapids.

GOODENOUGH, Ward Hunt

1963 *Cooperation in Change*, Russell Sage Foundation, New York.

GRANT, Robert M.

1972 *Early Christianity and Society*, Harper & Row, New York.

GREELEY, Andrew M.

1972 *The Denominational Society: A Sociological Approach to Religion in America*, Scott, Foresman and

        Company, Glenview, Illinois.

    1974 *Ethnicity in the United States,* John Wiley and Sons,
        New York.

    1975 *Why Can't They Be Like Us?,* E. P. Dutton & Co., New
        York.

GREEN, Hollis L.

    1972 *Why Churches Die,* Bethany Fellowship, Inc., Minne-
        apolis.

    1975 *Why Wait til Sunday,* Bethany Fellowship, Inc., Min-
        neapolis.

GRIFFITHS, Michael

    1975 *God's Forgetful Pilgrims,* Eerdmans, Grand Rapids.

GROSS, Llewellyn

    1967 *Sociological Theory: Inquiries and Paradigms,* Har-
        per & Row, New York.

HALDANE, Jean M., Nancy B. Geyer, James C. Fenhagen, James
D. Anderson and H. Barry Evans

    1973 *Prescriptions for Parishes,* The Seabury Press, New
        York.

HALE, J. Russell

    1978 *Who are the Unchurched?,* Glenmary Research
        Center, Washington, D.C.

    1980 *The Unchurched: Who They Are and Why They Stay
        Away,* Harper & Row, San Francisco.

HALL, J.

    1969 *Systems Maintenance: Gatekeeping and the Involve-
        ment Process,* Teleometrics International, Monroe,
        Texas.

HANDY, Robert T.

    1976 "American Pluriformity and Growth Toward Chris-
        tian Unity," *Mid-Stream,* vol. 15.

    1977 *A History of the Churches in the United States and
        Canada,* Oxford University Press, New York.

HARTMAN, Doug and Doug Sutherland

    1976 *A Guidebook to Discipleship,* Harvest House Pub-
        lishers, Irvine, California.

HARTMAN, Warren

    1976 *Membership Trends: A Study of Decline and Growth
        in the United Methodist Church 1949-1975,* Disci-
        pleship Resources, Nashville.

HAVLIK, John F.
    1976 *The Evangelistic Church,* Convention Press, Nash-
         ville.
HEFLEY, James C.
    1977 *Unique Evangelical Churches,* Word Books, Waco.
HEMBREE, Charles R.
    1975 *The Westside Story,* New Hope Press, Grand Rapids.
HENRICHSEN, Walter A.
    1975 *Disciples Are Made—Not Born,* Victor Books, Whea-
         ton.
HESS, Margaret and Bartlett Hess
    1977 *The Power of a Loving Church,* Regal Books, Glen-
         dale.
HESSELGRAVE, David J., ed.
    1980 *New Horizons in World Mission,* Baker, Grand
         Rapids.
HILLIS, Don
    1977 "Is America Over-Evangelized!," *Christianity To-
         day,* May 20.
HOCKING, David L.
    1976 *The World's Greatest Church,* Sounds of Grace,
         Long Beach, California.
HODGES, Melvin L.
    1970a *Growing Young Churches: How to Advance Indig-
          enous Churches Today,* Moody, Chicago.
    1970b "Surmounting Seven Obstacles to Church Growth,"
          Church Growth Bulletin, January.
HOEKSTRA, Harvey
    1979 *The World Council of Churches and the Demise of
         Evangelism,* Tyndale, Wheaton.
HOGE, Dean R. and David A. Roozen, eds.
    1979 *Understanding Church Growth and Decline: 1950-
         1978,* Pilgrim Press, New York.
HOGUE, C. B.
    1977 *I Want My Church to Grow,* Broadman, Nashville.
HUBER, Evelyn M.
    1975 *Enlist, Train, Support Church Leaders,* Judson
         Press, Valley Forge.
HUDNUT, Robert K.
    1975 *Church Growth is Not the Point,* Harper & Row, New
         York.

HUDSON, Winthrop S.
    1970 *Nationalism and Religion in America,* Harper &
    Row, New York.
HUNT, George L. and Paul A. Crow, Jr., eds.
    1965 *Where We Are in Church Union,* Association Press,
    New York.
HUNTER, George G., III
    1979 *The Contagious Congregation,* Abingdon, Nash-
    ville.
IRWIN, Leonard
    1976 *Supplemental Data: Churches and Church Member-
    ship in the U.S.,* Home Mission Board, Southern
    Baptist Convention, Atlanta.
JACQUET, Constant H., ed
    1980 *Yearbook of American and Canadian Churches,* Ab-
    ingdon, Nashville.
JEWETT, Paul K.
    1979 Lecture on Comparative Polity at Fuller Theological
    Seminary, Pasadena.
JOHNSON, David W. and Frank P. Johnson
    1975 *Joining Together—Group Theory and Group Skills,*
    Prentice-Hall, Englewood Cliffs, New Jersey.
JOHNSON, Douglas W.
    1978 *The Care & Feeding of Volunteers,* Abingdon, Nash-
    ville.
JOHNSON, Douglas W., Paul R. Picard and Bernard Quinn
    1971 *Churches and Church Membership in the United
    States,* Glenmary Research Center, Washington,
    D.C.
JOHNSON, Merle Allison
    1979 *How to be Happy in the Non-Electric Church,* Abing-
    don, Nashville.
JOHNSTON, Arthur P.
    1978 *Battle for World Evangelism,* Tyndale, Wheaton.
JONES, Ezra Earl
    1976 *Strategies for New Churches,* Harper & Row, New
    York.
JONES, Ezra Earl and Robert L. Wilson
    1974 *What's Ahead for Old First Church?,* Harper & Row,
    New York.

JUDY, Marvin T.
   1973   *The Parish Development Process*, Abingdon, Nash-
          ville.
KASTENS, Merritt
   1976   *Long Range Planning for Your Business*, Amacon,
          New York.
KEE, Howard Clark
   1980   *Christian Origins in Sociological Perspective*, West-
          minster, Philadelphia.
KELLEY, Dean M.
   1972   *Why Conservative Churches Are Growing: A Study
          in Sociology of Religion*, Harper & Row, New York.
KELSEY, David H.
   1975   *The Uses of Scripture in Recent Theology*, Fortress
          Press, Philadelphia.
KEMP, Charles F.
   1974   *Prayer-Based Growth Groups*, Abingdon, Nashville.
KEMPER, Robert
   1978   *Beginning a New Pastorate*, Abingdon, Nashville.
KILINSKI, Kenneth and Jerry Wofford
   1973   *Organization and Leadership in the Local Church*,
          Zondervan, Grand Rapids.
KOLB, Erwin J.
   1977   "Save Us From Synergism," *Concordia Journal*, vol.
          3, July.
KRAFT, Charles H.
   1963   "Christian Conversion or Cultural Conversion,"
          Practical Anthropology, vol. 10.
   1973a "God's Model for Cross-Cultural Communication,"
          Evangelical Missions Quarterly, vol. 9, Summer.
   1973b "Toward a Christian Ethnotheology," *God, Man and
          Church Growth*, Alan R. Tippett, ed., Eerdmans,
          Grand Rapids.
   1973c "North America's Cultural Challenge," *Christianity
          Today*, vol. 27.
   1977a "The Essence of Syncretism," lecture given in Ad-
          vanced Ethnotheology Course at Fuller Theological
          Seminary, Pasadena.
   1977b *Theologizing In Culture*, pre-publication draft of
          Christianity in Culture (1979), Fuller Theological

Seminary, Pasadena.

1979 *Christianity in Culture: A Study in Dynamic Theologizing in Cross-Cultural Perspective,* Orbis, Maryknoll.

KRAUS, C. Norman, ed.

1980 *Missions, Evangelism and Church Growth,* Herald Press, Scottdale, Pennsylvania.

KUHN, Alfred

1974 *The Logic of Systems,* Jossey-Bass Publishers, San Francisco.

KUHN, Thomas S.

1962 *The Structure of Scientific Revolutions,* University of Chicago, Chicago.

KUNG, Hans

1967 *The Church,* Sheed & Ward, New York.

1978a *Contemporary Issues Facing the Church,* Doubleday, New York.

1978b *Signposts for the Future,* Doubleday, New York.

KUNG, Hans, ed.

1972 *Post-Ecumenical Christianity,* Herder & Herder, New York.

KUNG, Hans and Walter Kasper, eds.

1973 *Polarization in the Church,* Herder & Herder, New York.

LABORIT, Henri

1977 *Decoding the Human Message,* St. Martin's Press, New York.

LADD, George Eldon

1975 *The Gospel of the Kingdom,* Eerdmans, Grand Rapids.

LAMBERT, Norman M.

1975 *Managing Church Groups,* Pflaum Publishing, Dayton, Ohio.

LARSON, Bruce and Ralph Osborne

1970 *The Emerging Church,* Word Books, Waco.

LAWSON, E. LeRoy and Tetsunao Yamamori

1975 *Church Growth: Everybody's Business,* Standard, Cincinnati.

LEBSACK, Lee

1974 *Ten at the Top,* New Hope Press, Stow, Ohio.

LESLIE, Robert C.
    1970 *Sharing Groups in the Church,* Abingdon, Nashville.
LEWIS, G. Douglass
    1975 "Building and Sustaining Community: An Over-
        view," *Building and Sustaining Community,* Educa-
        tional Systems & Designs, Inc., Westport, Connecti-
        cut.
LIEFFER, Murray H.
    1955 *The Effective City Church,* Abingdon, Nashville.
LINCOLN, C. Eric
    1975 "Americanity: The Third Force in American Plural-
        ism," *Religious Education,* vol. 70.
LINDGREN, Alvin J. and Norman Shawchuck
    1977 *Management for Your Church,* Abingdon, Nashville.
LIPPITT, Gordon and Ronald Lippitt
    1978 *The Consulting Process in Action,* University Asso-
        ciates, La Jolla, California.
LIPPITT, Ronald
    1958 *The Dynamics of Planned Change,* Harcourt, Brace
        and World, Inc., New York.
LOEWEN, Jacob A.
    1975 *Culture and Human Values: Christian Intervention
        in Anthropological Perspective,* William Carey,
        Pasadena.
LONGENECKER, Harold
    1973 *Building Town and Country Churches,* Moody, Chi-
        cago.
LUZBETAK, Louis J.
    1970 *The Church and Cultures,* Divine Word Publications,
        Techny, Illinois.
LYON, William
    1977 *A Pew for One Please,* The Seabury Press, New York.
MACKIE, Steven G., ed.
    1970 *Can Churches Be Compared?,* Friendship Press, New
        York.
McBETH, Leon
    1968 *The First Baptist Church of Dallas,* Zondervan,
        Grand Rapids.
McDONOUGH, Reginald
    1975 *Leading Your Church in Long Range Planning,* Con-
        vention Press, Nashville.

McFADDEN, Thomas M., ed.
    1976 *America in Theological Perspective,* The Seabury Press, New York.

McGAVRAN, Donald
    1955 *The Bridges of God,* Friendship Press, New York.
    1970 *Understanding Church Growth,* Eerdmans, Grand Rapids.
    1974 "How to Do a Survey of Church Growth," in A. Martin's *The Means of World Evangelization,* William Carey, Pasadena.
    1976b Letter to David Barrett, November 29, distributed to doctoral candidates at Fuller Theological Seminary, Pasadena.
    1977a "Seven Missiological Streams," unpublished article distributed to Advanced Church Growth Course at Fuller Theological Seminary, Pasadena.
    1977b "The Current Conciliar Theology of Mission," lecture in Contemporary Theology Course at Fuller Theological Seminary, Pasadena.
    (Battery sequence is collated with McGavran, ed., below.)
    1977d "The Nature of Mission," lecture in Advanced Church Growth Course at Fuller Theological Seminary, Pasadena.
    1977e "What is Mission?" unpublished article distributed to Contemporary Theology Course at Fuller Theological Seminary, Pasadena.
    1977g "Making Doctrines More Biblically Accurate and Missionarily Effective," unpublished article distributed at Conference on Contemporary Theology at Fuller Theological Seminary, Pasadena.
    1979a *Ethnic Realities and the Church,* William Carey, Pasadena.
    1979b "How About that New Verb 'to Disciple?,' " *Church Growth Bulletin,* May.

McGAVRAN, Donald and Winfield C. Arn
    1973 *How to Grow a Church,* Regal Books, Glendale.
    1977 *Ten Steps for Church Growth,* Harper & Row, San Francisco.

McGAVRAN, Donald and George G. Hunter
  1980 *Church Growth Strategies that Work*, Abingdon, Nashville.
McGAVRAN, Donald, ed.
  1969 *Church Growth Bulletin: Vol. I-V*, William Carey, Pasadena.
  1972 *Crucial Issues in Missions Tomorrow*, Moody, Chicago.
  1976a *Church Growth and Christian Mission*, William Carey, Pasadena.
  1977c *Church Growth Bulletin: Vol. VI-X*, William Carey, Pasadena.
  1977f *The Conciliar-Evangelical Debate: the Crucial Documents, 1964-1976*, William Carey, Pasadena.
McGUINNIS, Allen
  1979 *The Friendship Factor*, Augsburg, Minneapolis.
McINTIRE, C. T., ed.
  1977 *God, History and Historians*, Oxford University Press, New York.
McLOUGHLIN, William G.
  1978 *Revivals, Awakenings, and Reforms*, University of Chicago, Chicago.
McNAMARA, Patrick H., ed.
  1974 *Religion American Style*, Harper & Row, New York.
McPHEE, Arthur G.
  1978 *Friendship Evangelism: The Caring Way to Share Your Faith*, Zondervan, Grand Rapids.
McQUILKIN, J. Robertson
  1974 *Measuring the Church Growth Movement, How Biblical is It?*, Moody, Chicago.
MADSEN, Paul O.
  1975 *The Small Church: Valid, Vital, Victorious*, Judson Press, Valley Forge.
MAINS, David
  1971 *Full Circle*, Word Books, Waco.
MALLISON, John
  1978 *Building Small Groups in the Christian Community*, Renewal Publications, West Ryde, Australia.
MARCUM, Elvis
  1975 *Outreach: God's Miracle Business*, Broadman, Nashville.

MARTIN, Alvin, ed.
   1974 *The Means of World Evangelization: Missiological Education at the Fuller School of World Mission*, William Carey, Pasadena.
MARTIN, Dan
   1977 "The Church Growth Questions," Southern Baptist *Home Missions*, December.
MARTIN, Ralph P.
   1980 *The Family and the Fellowship: New Testament Images of the Church*, Eerdmans, Grand Rapids.
MARTY, Martin
   1976 *A Nation of Behavers*, University of Chicago, Chicago.
MAYERS, Marvin K.
   1974 *Christianity Confronts Culture: A Strategy for Cross-Cultural Evangelism*, Zondervan, Grand Rapids.
MEAD, Frank S.
   1975 *Handbook of Denominations in the United States*, Abingdon, Nashville.
MEHAN, Hugh and Houston Wood
   1975 *The Reality of Ethnomethodology*, John Wiley and Sons, New York.
MELTON, J. Gordon
   1978 *Directory of Religious Bodies in the United States*, Institute for the Study of Religion, Evanston, Illinois.
METZ, Donald L.
   1967 *New Congregations*, Westminster, Philadelphia.
METZ, Rene and Jean Schlick
   1975 *Informal Groups in the Church*, The Pickwick Press, Pittsburgh.
MINOR, Harold D.
   1972 *Finding and Training Leaders in the Local Church*, Board of Education, United Methodist Church, Nashville.
MITCHELL, Henry
   1975 *Black Belief*, Harper & Row, San Francisco.
MOBERG, David O.
   1962 *The Church As a Social Institution*, Prentice-Hall, Englewood Cliffs, New Jersey.

1972 *The Great Reversal: Evangelism versus Social Concern*, J. B. Lippincott Co., Philadelphia.

MOORE, John
1978 "New Wine in Portland," *Eternity*, August.

MOORHOUS, Carl W.
1975 *Growing New Churches*, Chicago District Evangelistic Assn., Harvey, Illinois.

MURPHY, Edward F.
1975 *Spiritual Gifts and the Great Commission*, William Carey, Pasadena.

MYLANDER, Charles E.
1975 *Suburban Friends Church Growth in Southern California*, unpublished doctor of ministry thesis, Fuller Theological Seminary, Pasadena.
1979 *Secrets for Growing Churches*, Harper & Row, New York.

MYRDAL, Gunnar
1969 *Objectivity in Social Research*, Pantheon Books, New York.

NEIGHBOUR, Ralph W.
1972 *The Seven Last Words of the Church: We Never Did it That Way Before*, Zondervan, Grand Rapids.
1975 *Target Group Evangelism*, Broadman, Nashville.

NEILL, Stephen, Gerald H. Anderson and John Goodwin, eds.
1971 *Concise Dictionary of the Christian World Mission*, Abingdon, Nashville.

NIDA, Eugene A.
1960 *Message and Mission: The Communication of the Christian Faith*, William Carey, Pasadena.
1976 "Dynamics of Church Growth," *Church Growth and Christian Mission*, Donald McGavran, ed., William Carey, Pasadena.

NISBET, Robert A.
1970 *The Social Bond*, Alfred A. Knopf, New York.

NOVAK, Michael
1973 *The Rise of the Unmeltable Ethnics*, Macmillan, New York.

NOYCE, Gaylord
1973 *Survival and Mission for the City Church*, Westminster, Philadelphia.

O'CONNOR, Elizabeth
    1976 *The New Community,* Harper & Row, New York.
O'DEA, Thomas F.
    1966 *The Sociology of Religion,* Prentice-Hall, Englewood
        Cliffs, New Jersey.
ODEN, Thomas C.
    1972 *The Intensive Group Experience: The New Pietism,*
        Westminster, Philadelphia.
OLIVER, Dennis
    1973 *Making Disciples: The Nature & Scope of the Great
        Commission,* unpublished doctor of missiology
        thesis, Fuller Theological Seminary, Pasadena.
OLSEN, Charles M.
    1973 *The Base Church,* Forum House, Atlanta.
ORJALA, Paul R.
    1978 *Get Ready to Grow,* Beacon Hill Press, Kansas City.
ORR, J. Edwin
    1973a "Evangelical Dynamic and Social Action," *God,
        Man & Church Growth,* Alan R. Tippett, ed., Eerd-
        mans, Grand Rapids.
    1973b *The Flaming Tongue,* Moody, Chicago.
    1974 *The Fervent Prayer,* Moody, Chicago.
    1975 *The Eager Feet,* Moody, Chicago.
OSBORNE, Ronald
        "Religious Freedom and the Form of the Church:
        An Assessment of the Denomination in America,"
        Lexington Theological Quarterly, vol. 11.
PADILLA, C. Rene
    1976 *The New Face of Evangelicalism,* Inter-Varsity,
        Downers Grove.
PALMER, Bernard and Marjorie Palmer
    1976 *How Churches Grow,* Bethany Fellowship, Inc., Min-
        neapolis.
PARSEGIAN, V. L.
    1973 "Biological Trends within the Cosmic Process," *Zy-
        gon,* vol. 8.
PERRY, Lloyd
    1977 *Getting the Church on Target,* Moody, Chicago.
PETERS, George W.
    1972 *A Biblical Theology of Missions,* Moody, Chicago.

PETERSEN, William J., ed.
    1978 "Twenty-five New Church Ideas," *Eternity*, August.
PIEPKORN, Arthur C.
    1977 *Roman Catholic, Old Catholic and Eastern Orthodox Bodies, Profiles in Belief*, vol. I, Harper & Row, New York.
    1978 *Protestant Denominations, Profiles in Belief*, vol. II, Harper & Row, New York.
    1979 *Holiness and Pentecostal, Evangelical, Fundamentalist and Other Christian Bodies, Profiles in Belief*, vol. III-IV, Harper & Row, New York.
POTTER, Burt
    1976 *The Church Reaching Out*, Moore Publishing Company, Durham, North Carolina.
QUEBEDEAUX, Richard
    1976 *The New Charismatics: The Origins, Development and Significance of New-Pentecostalism*, Harper & Row, New York.
    1978 *The Worldly Evangelicals*, Harper & Row, San Francisco.
RAGSDALE, Ray
    1978 *The Mid-Life Crises of a Minister*, Word Books, Waco.
RAHNER, Karl
    1964 *The Christian in the Market Place*, Sheed & Ward, New York.
RAUFF, Edward A.
    1979 *Why People Join the Church*, Pilgrim Press, New York.
READ, William R., Victor M. Monterroso and Harmon A. Johnson
    1969 *Latin American Church Growth*, Eerdmans, Grand Rapids.
REDDIN, William J.
    1970 *Managerial Effectiveness*, McGraw-Hill, New York.
REDFORD, Jack
    1978 *Planting New Churches*, Broadman, Nashville.
REED, Millard
    1977 *Let Your Church Grow*, Beacon Hill Press, Kansas City.
REEVES, R. Daniel
    1977a "The Relationship Between Pluralism and Polariza-

tion: A Case for the Legitimacy of American Ethnic Theologies," an unpublished article on ethnotheology.

1977b "What a Biblical Theology of Mission Does," *Church Growth Bulletin,* September.

1977c "Ecumenicism and the World Council of Churches in America," an unpublished article on ecumenics.

1977d "Pathways to Growth," *Church Growth: America,* Summer.

REUDI-WEBER, Hans

1959 "The Marks of an Evangelizing Church," *The Missionary Church in East and West,* SCM Press, London.

RICHARDS, Lawrence O.

1975 *Three Churches in Renewal,* Zondervan, Grand Rapids.

RICHEY, Russell E., ed.

1977 *Denominationalism,* Abingdon, Nashville.

ROMERO, Joel

1973 "Symbolism and Syncretism," *God, Man and Church Growth,* Alan R. Tippett, ed., Eerdmans, Grand Rapids.

ROOZEN, David A.

1978 *The Churched and the Unchurched in America,* Glenmary Research Center, Washington, D.C.

ROUSE, Ruth and Stephen Charles Neill, eds.

1967 *A History of the Ecumenical Movement, 1517-1948,* Westminster, Philadelphia.

RUSBULDT, Richard E., Richard K. Gladden and Norman M. Green

1977 *Local Church Planning Manual,* Judson Press, Valley Forge.

RYALS, Delane M.

1979 "The Types of Churches," *The Birth of Churches,* Talmadge Amberson, ed., Broadman, Nashville.

SARASON, Seymour B.

1972 *The Creation of Settings and the Future Societies,* Jossey-Bass Publishers, San Francisco.

SAVAGE, John S.

1976 *The Apathetic and Bored Church Member,* Lead Consultants, Pittsford, New York.

SCHALLER, Lyle E.

1968 *The Local Church Looks to the Future*, Abingdon, Nashville.

1972 *The Change Agent: The Strategy of Innovative Leadership*, Abingdon, Nashville.

1975a *Hey, That's Our Church!*, Abingdon, Nashville.

1975b "Seven Characteristics of Growing Churches," *Church Administration*, October.

1977 *Survival Tactics in the Parish*, Abingdon, Nashville.

1978 *Assimilating New Members*, Creative Leadership Series, Abingdon, Nashville.

1979 *Effective Church Planning*, Abingdon, Nashville.

1980 *The Multiple Staff and the Larger Church*, Abingdon, Nashville.

SCHALLER, Lyle E. and Charles A. Tidwell

1975 *Creative Church Administration*, Abingdon, Nashville.

SCHELLING, Thomas C.

1978 *Micromotives and Macrobehavior*, Norton and Co., New York.

SCHILS, Edward

1975 *Center and Periphery: Essays in Macrosociology*, University of Chicago, Chicago.

SCHULLER, David S., Merton P. Strommen and Milo L. Brekke, eds.

1980 *Ministry in America*, Harper & Row, San Francisco.

SCHULLER, Robert H.

1975 *Your Church Has Real Possibilities*, Regal Books, Glendale.

SCHUMACHER, E. F.

1973 *Small Is Beautiful: Economics as if People Mattered*, Harper & Row, New York.

SHANNON, Foster H.

1977 *The Growth Crisis in the American Church: A Presbyterian Case Study*, William Carey, Pasadena.

SHAPIRO, Deanne Ruth

1976 "The New Ethnicity: Myth or Reality," *Foundations*, vol. 19.

SHAWCHUCK, Norman, Robert C. Worley, G. Douglas Lewis and

H. Rhea Gray
    1977 *Experiences in Activating Congregations,* Westminster, Philadelphia.
SHENK, Wilbert R., ed.
    1973 *The Challenge of Church Growth: A Symposium,* Herald Press, Scottdale, Pennsylvania.
SHEPARD, C. E.
    1969 *New Church Evangelism,* Mission Services Press, Kempton, Indiana.
SHEPHERD, Jack F.
    1973 "Continuity and Change in Christian Mission," *God, Man and Church Growth,* Alan R. Tippett, ed., Eerdmans, Grand Rapids.
SIMKINS, Cyril Curtis
    1977 *The Expansion of the Church in Luke's Writing,* unpublished doctor of missiology thesis, Fuller Theological Seminary, Pasadena.
SIZEMORE, Burlan A.
    1976 "Christian Faith in a Pluralistic World," *Journal of Ecumenical Studies,* Summer.
SKELTON, Eugene
    1974 *Ten Fastest-Growing Southern Baptist Sunday Schools,* Broadman, Nashville.
SMITH, Ebbie C.
    1976 *A Manual for Church Growth Surveys,* William Carey, Pasadena.
SNYDER, Howard A.
    1976 *The Problem of Wine Skins: Church Structure in a Technological Age,* Inter-Varsity, Downers Grove.
SPITTLER, Russell P., ed.
    1976 *Perspectives on the New Pentecostalism,* Baker, Grand Rapids.
STARR, Timothy
    1978 *Church Planting: Always in Season,* Fellowship of Evangelical Baptist Churches in Canada, Willowdale, Ontario.
STEDMAN, Ray C.
    1972 *Body Life,* Regal Books, Glendale.
STEEMAN, Theodore M.
    1974 "Religious Pluralism and National Integration,"

Harvard Theological Review, vol. 67.

STOTT, John R. W.

   1975 *Christian Mission in the Modern World,* Inter-Varsity, Downers Grove.

SWEAZEY, George E.

   1978 *The Church as Evangelist,* Harper & Row, San Francisco.

SWEET, William Warren

   1953 *Methodism in American History,* Abingdon, New York.

Te SELLE, Sallie, ed.

   1973 *The Rediscovery of Ethnicity,* Harper & Row, New York.

TIPPETT, Alan R.

   1965 "Numbering: Right or Wrong?," *Church Growth Bulletin,* vol. 1.

   1967 *Solomon Islands Christianity: A Study in Growth and Obstruction,* William Carey, Pasadena.

   1970 *Church Growth and the Word of God,* Eerdmans, Grand Rapids.

   1973b *Verdict Theology in Missionary Theory,* William Carey, Pasadena.

   1974 "Research Method and the Missiological Process," *The Means of World Evangelization,* Alvin Martin, ed., William Carey, Pasadena.

TIPPETT, Alan R., ed.

   1973a *God, Man and Church Growth,* Eerdmans, Grand Rapids.

TOON, Peter

   1979 *The Development of Doctrine in the Church,* Eerdmans, Grand Rapids.

TOWNS, Elmer

   1972 *America's Fastest Growing Churches,* Impact, Nashville.

   1973 *Great Soul-Winning Churches,* Sword of the Lord Publishers, Murfreesboro, Tennessee.

   1974 *World's Largest Sunday School,* Thomas Nelson, Inc., Nashville.

   1975 *Getting a Church Started in the Face of Insurmountable Odds with Limited Resources in Unlikely Cir-*

cumstances, Impact Books, Nashville.
TUCKER, Michael
   1978 *The Church: Change or Decay,* Tyndale, Wheaton.
TURNEY-HIGH, Harry Holbert
   1968 *Man and System,* Appleton-Century-Crofts, Inc., New York.
ULLMANN-MARGALIT, Edna
   1977 *The Emergence of Norms,* Clarendon Press, Oxford.
VAN DEUSEN, Henry P.
   1961 *One Great Ground of Hope,* Westminster, Philadelphia.
VERKUYL, Johannes
   1978 *Contemporary Missiology: An Introduction,* Eerdmans, Grand Rapids.
VUILLEUMIER, Marion Rawson and Pierre Dupont Vuilleumier
   1976 *America's Religious Treasures,* Harper & Row, New York.
WADDINGTON, C. H.
   1977 *Tools for Thought,* Basic Books, Inc., New York.
WAGNER, C. Peter
   1971 *Frontiers in Missionary Strategy,* Moody, Chicago.
   1973a "'Church Growth:' More Than a Man, a Magazine, a School, a Book," *Christianity Today,* December 7.
   1973b *Look Out! The Pentecostals are Coming,* Creation House, Carol Stream, Illinois.
   1975 "The Stott-Wagner Debate," lecture given in Missions Strategy Course at Fuller Theological Seminary, Pasadena.
   1976 *Your Church Can Grow,* Regal Books, Glendale.
   1979a *Your Spiritual Gifts Can Help Your Church Grow,* Regal Books, Glendale.
   1979b *Our Kind of People,* John Knox Press, Atlanta.
   1979c *Your Church Can Be Healthy,* Abingdon, Nashville.
   1979d "Church Growth Research: the Paradigm and Its Application," *Understanding Church Growth and Decline,* Dean Hoge and David Roozen, eds., Pilgrim Press, New York.
WAGNER, C. Peter, ed.
   1972 *Church Mission Tensions Today,* Moody, Chicago.
WAGNER, C. Peter and Edward R. Dayton, eds.

1979 *Unreached Peoples '79,* David C. Cook, Elgin, Illinois.

WALLACE, Anthony F.C.
1966 *Religion: an Anthropological View,* Random House, New York.

WALRATH, Douglas W.
1977 "Types of Small Congregations and Their Implications for Planning," *Small Churches Are Beautiful,* Jackson W. Carroll, ed., Harper & Row, San Francisco.

WALRATH, Douglas Alan
1979 *Leading Churches Through Change,* Abingdon, Nashville.

WARREN, Roland L.
1965 *Studying Your Community,* Russell Sage Foundation, New York.

WATSON, E. O.
1923 *Yearbook of the Churches,* Federal Council of Churches, New York.

WAYMIRE, Bob and C. Peter Wagner
1980 *The Church Growth Survey Handbook,* Global Church Growth Bulletin, Santa Clara, California.

WERNING, Waldo J.
1977 *Vision and Strategy for Church Growth,* Moody, Chicago.

WHEELEY, B. Otto
1975 *Church Planning and Management: A Guide for Pastors and Laymen,* Dorrance & Company, Philadelphia.

WILLIAMS, Walter and Richard F. Elmore, eds.
1976 *Social Program Implementation,* Academic Press, New York.

WILLIAMSON, Wayne G.
1979 *Growth & Decline in the Episcopal Church,* William Carey, Pasadena.

WIMBER, John
1976 "People Flow to Maturity," concepts developed in consulting work at Fuller Evangelistic Association, Pasadena.
1977 "Finding the Functionally Unchurched," chart

                    developed for Fuller Evangelistic Association
                    denominational training, Pasadena.
WINTER, Ralph D.
        1972 "Quality or Quantity," *Crucial Issues in Missions
                    Tomorrow,* Donald McGavran, ed., Moody, Chicago.
        1974a "Milestone Books in the Church Growth Move-
                    ment," A. Martin's *The Means of World Evangeliza-
                    tion,* William Carey, Pasadena.
        1974b "Seeing the Task Graphically," *Evangelical Mis-
                    sions Quarterly,* January.
        1974c "The Two Structures of God's Redemptive Mission,"
                    Missiology April.
        1975 "The Highest Priority: Cross Cultural Evangelism,"
                    Let the Earth Hear His Voice, World Wide Publica-
                    tions, Minneapolis.
        1978 *Penetrating the Last Frontiers,* U.S. Center for World
                    Mission, Pasadena.
WINTER, Ralph D. and R. Pierce Beaver
        1970 *The Warp and the Woof,* William Carey, Pasadena.
WOLLEN, Albert J.
        1976 *Miracles Happen in Group Bible Study,* Regal Books,
                    Glendale.
WOODBRIDGE, John D.
        1975 *The Evangelicals: What They Believe, Who They Are,
                    Where They Are Changing,* Abingdon, Nashville.
WORKS, Herbert Melvin
        1974 *The Church Growth Movement to 1965,* a doctor of
                    missiology thesis at the School of World Mission,
                    Pasadena.
WORLEY, Robert C.
        1976 *A Gathering of Strangers: Understanding the Life
                    of Your Church,* Westminster, Philadelphia.
YAMAMORI, Tetsunao and LeRoy Lawson
        1975 *Introducing Church Growth,* Standard, Cincinnati.
YAMAMORI, Tetsunao and charles Taber, eds.
        1975 *Christopaganism or Indigenous Christianity,* Wil-
                    liam Carey, Pasadena.
YEAKLEY, Flavil R.
        1977 *Why Churches Grow,* Anderson's, Nashville.
YINGER, J. Milton

1970 *The Scientific Study of Religion,* Collier-Macmillan, London.

YODER, Don Herbert
1967 "Christian Unity in Nineteenth-Century America," *A History of the Ecumenical Movement 1517-1948,* Ruth Rouse and Stephen Neil, eds., Westminister, Philadelphia.

YOHN, Rick
1975 *Discover Your Spiritual Gift and Use It,* Tyndale, Wheaton.

ZARETSKY, Irving I. and Mark P. Leone, eds.
1974 *Religious Movements in Contemporary America,* Princeton University Press, Princeton, New Jersey.

ZIEGENHALS, Walter E.
1978 *Urban Churches in Transition,* Pilgrim Press, New York.

ZIMBARDO, Philip and Ebbe B. Ebbeson
1970 *Influencing Attitudes and Changing Behavior,* Addison-Wesley Publishing, Reading, Massachusetts.

INDEX OF PERSONS

INDEX OF SUBJECTS